Unified Protocol
for Transdiagnostic Treatment
of Emotional Disorders
in Children

Unified Protocol for Transdiagnostic Treatment of Emotional Disorders in Children

WORKBOOK

JILL EHRENREICH-MAY

SARAH M. KENNEDY

JAMIE A. SHERMAN

EMILY L. BILEK

DAVID H. BARLOW

ILLUSTRATIONS BY STEFANIA S. PINTO

OXFORD
UNIVERSITY PRESS

OXFORD
UNIVERSITY PRESS

Oxford University Press is a department of the University of Oxford. It furthers
the University's objective of excellence in research, scholarship, and education
by publishing worldwide. Oxford is a registered trade mark of Oxford University
Press in the UK and certain other countries.

Published in the United States of America by Oxford University Press
198 Madison Avenue, New York, NY 10016, United States of America.

ISBN 978–0–19–064295–2

One of the most difficult problems confronting the parents of children with various disorders and diseases is finding the best help available. Everyone is aware of friends or family who have sought treatment from a seemingly reputable practitioner, only to find out later from another doctor that the original diagnosis was wrong or the treatments recommended were inappropriate or perhaps even harmful. Most parents or family members address this problem by reading everything they can about their children's symptoms, seeking out information on the Internet, or aggressively asking around to tap knowledge from friends and acquaintances. Governments and health care policymakers are also aware that people in need don't always get the best treatments—something they refer to as "variability in health care practices."

Now health care systems around the world are attempting to correct this variability by introducing "evidence-based practice." This simply means that it is in everyone's interest that patients of all ages get the most up-to-date and effective care for a particular problem. Health care policymakers have also recognized that it is very useful to give consumers of health care as much information as possible, so that they can make intelligent decisions in a collaborative effort to improve health and mental health. This series, Programs *ThatWork*™, is designed to accomplish just that for children suffering from behavioral health problems. Only the latest and most effective interventions for particular problems are described in user-friendly language. To be included in this series, each treatment program must pass the highest standards of evidence available, as determined by a scientific advisory board. Thus, when parents with children suffering from these problems or their family members seek out an expert clinician who is familiar with these interventions and decide that they are appropriate, they will have confidence that they are receiving the best care available. Of course, only your health care professional can decide on the right mix of treatments for your child.

This workbook is designed to help your child learn to manage strong emotions more effectively at home. It outlines a program to better the lives of your child and your family, and is most effective for children between

7 and 13 years of age. This program was developed by some of the foremost experts on emotional disorders in children, and has significant scientific support. The program is most effectively applied by working in collaboration with your child's clinician.

Anne Marie Albano, Editor-in-Chief
David H. Barlow, Editor-in-Chief
Programs *ThatWork*

Accessing Programs *ThatWork* Forms and Worksheets Online

All forms and worksheets from books in the PTW series are made available digitally shortly following print publication. You may download, print, save, and digitally complete them as PDFs. To access the forms and worksheets, please visit http://www.oup.com/us/ttw.

Contents

Introduction to the *Unified Protocol for Transdiagnostic Treatment of Emotional Disorders in Children: Workbook* for Parents   ix

Unified Protocol for Transdiagnostic Treatment of Emotional Disorders in Children: Welcome for Children   1

Chapter 1   C Skill: Consider How I Feel (Session 1)   3

Chapter 2   C Skill: Consider How I Feel (Session 2)   11

Chapter 3   C Skill: Consider How I Feel (Session 3)   19

Chapter 4   C Skill: Consider How I Feel (Session 4)   29

Chapter 5   L Skill: Look at My Thoughts (Session 5)   37

Chapter 6   U Skill: Use Detective Thinking and Problem Solving
                (Session 6)   45

Chapter 7   U Skill: Use Detective Thinking and Problem Solving
                (Session 7)   53

Chapter 8   E Skill: Experience My Emotions (Session 8)   61

Chapter 9   E Skill: Experience My Emotions (Session 9)   67

Chapter 10   E Skill: Experience My Emotions (Session 10)   73

Chapter 11   E Skill: Experience My Emotions (Sessions 11–14)   79

Chapter 12   S Skill: Stay Healthy and Happy (Session 15)   87

Chapter 13   Consider How I Feel for Parents (Sessions 1–4
              for Parents)   *93*

Chapter 14   Look at My Thoughts for Parents (Session 5
              for Parents)   *123*

Chapter 15   Use Detective Thinking and Problem Solving
              for Parents (Sessions 6 and 7 for Parents)   *133*

Chapter 16   Experience My Emotions for Parents (Sessions 8–14
              for Parents)   *155*

Chapter 17   Stay Healthy and Happy for Parents (Session 15
              for Parents)   *195*

About the Authors   *205*

Introduction to the *Unified Protocol for Transdiagnostic Treatment of Emotional Disorders in Children: Workbook* for Parents

Introduction Goals

■ To learn about who this program is for and the types of problems it addresses

■ To learn what to expect from this program

■ To learn how to help prepare your child for this program

Welcome to Treatment—UP-C Parents!

Hello, and welcome to the workbook for the *Unified Protocol for Transdiagnostic Treatment of Emotional Disorders in Children*! If you are reading this introduction, you are probably considering participating in this treatment program or are perhaps seeking some skills to help your child learn to manage strong emotions more effectively at home. If this sounds like you, we hope that the information, skills, and home learning assignments in this workbook will be helpful to you and your child. Parents often have many questions before beginning a treatment like this. We provide answers to some of the most common questions raised by parents in the pages of this introduction. Our hope is that these answers allow you to feel as prepared as possible for participating in this program. Although your child's emotions may sometimes seem quite mysterious to you, we don't want to leave you in suspense about what to expect from treatment. Once treatment is no longer a mystery to you, you can focus your effort and attention on helping your child solve the mystery of his or her emotions and become an "Emotion Detective."

Frequently Asked Questions

Is My Child Right for this Program?

This is a treatment for "emotional disorders" that is most appropriate for children between the ages of 7 and 13, although your child may be able to benefit if he or she is just outside this age range. If you are the parent of a teenager with an emotional disorder, we have another treatment within the Unified Protocol family—the *Unified Protocol for Transdiagnostic Treatment of Emotional Disorders in Adolescents*—that would likely be a better fit for you and your teen. In fact, there is another workbook available that is just for teens to use themselves, along with the UP-A.

You may be wondering at this point what an **emotional disorder** is. When we use that term in this treatment, we are referring to the experience of very frequent and strong emotions, and the distress that is felt about the experience of these negative emotions, often accompanied by efforts to quickly reduce, suppress, or avoid these emotions at all costs. Your child might be right for this treatment if he or she is experiencing any number of intense emotions typically thought of as negative or difficult to manage (such as sadness, anxiety, worry, irritability, frustration, anger, or guilt)—or even really low levels of emotions typically thought of as pleasant or positive in nature (such as joy and happiness)—and if these emotions (or lack thereof) are interfering with your child's ability to participate, succeed in, or enjoy day-to-day activities. This program may not be the right fit if your child's primary problem is difficulty focusing in school, having trouble learning, purposely breaking rules at home or at school, or having trouble sitting down for long periods of time.

What Will My Child Be Doing During this Treatment?

Many people think of therapy as a place for expressing emotions or talking about difficult experiences from the past. While your child may be doing these things from time to time during this treatment, your child will spend most of his or her time in treatment learning what we refer to as **Emotion Detective skills** to more effectively manage the types of emotions and situations that are a problem *right now* in your child's day-to-day life. Many of these skills are based on strategies and principles from a variety of different types of treatments for emotional disorders, including cognitive-behavioral therapy, behavioral therapy, and mindfulness and acceptance-based therapies. During sessions, your child will be participating in games, activities, and experiments to learn these skills and apply them to all different types of emotional situations.

What Makes this Treatment Different?

Many of the treatment programs or manuals out there today tend to introduce skills for coping with a single problem area or type of concern. For example, some treatments focus on reducing anxiety or perhaps some even more specific types of anxiety, such as panic attacks or social anxiety around other people. Other treatments focus primarily on reducing depression or on reducing the repetitive thoughts and behaviors commonly seen in obsessive-compulsive disorder. Even though most children (and adults too) tend to experience problems with emotions that cut across some of these categories, existing treatment programs don't always teach skills that are helpful for multiple problem areas or adequately explain how a skill can be applied to many different emotions. This is where the Unified Protocols—a transdiagnostic family of treatments targeting multiple disorders or problem areas with the same set of skills—come in. Your child will be learning a single set of Emotion Detective skills for becoming more aware of emotions, for tolerating emotions with less distress and discomfort, and for acting differently to what the emotion is telling your child to do (e.g., approaching situations that might make your child experience strong emotions and want to avoid). Your child can use this same set of Emotion Detective skills whether he or she is feeling sad, angry, anxious, bored, afraid, or some other emotion.

Is There Any Evidence That This Treatment Works?

Yes, absolutely! The *Unified Protocol for Transdiagnostic Treatment of Emotional Disorders in Children* (which we will refer to as UP-C for short) was developed at the University of Miami by experts in emotional disorders in the Child and Adolescent Mood and Anxiety Treatment (CAMAT) program. Both the UP-C and its sister program for adolescents (the UP-A) are based on the *Unified Protocol for Transdiagnostic Treatment of Emotional Disorders*, a treatment for adults developed by researchers and therapists at Boston University's Center for Anxiety and Related Disorders (CARD), led by David H. Barlow, PhD. Evidence from research studies and our clinical experiences suggests that UP-C and UP-A are quite effective in reducing the frequency and intensity of strong emotions in children and adolescents, respectively. About two-thirds of children who participate in the UP-C group program in our clinic are much or very much improved at the end of treatment, and about three-fourths of children are much or very much improved six months after treatment ends. If you and your child keep practicing your Emotion Detective skills at home after treatment ends, your child may continue to improve well into the future!

How Long Is Treatment? How Long Will It Take for My Child to Get Better?

The UP-C program is designed to be completed in 15 sessions. On average, research we have conducted in our clinic and research on cognitive-behavioral treatments in general has shown that most children achieve a significant and meaningful improvement in their symptoms in those 15 sessions. That being said, all children are different, and some children may require more sessions than this to achieve maximum improvement in their symptoms. In our experience, these additional sessions would most likely be spent focusing on something we call "emotion exposures," which involve (gradually) facing and sticking with situations that elicit difficult emotions. After your child completes this program, you may wish to talk with your child's therapist about whether your child might benefit from more than 15 sessions.

Before beginning this program, you should know that children vary greatly in when and how quickly they improve. Some parents notice improvements in their child's symptoms after just a few sessions of this program, and others may not notice improvements until closer to the end of treatment. Your child may also have an amazing week where he or she is able to use skills to approach and manage tough situations, followed by a week where a difficult event seems to set your child back. You should know that there is no one "right" path through treatment, and all children have ups and downs on the path to becoming skillful Emotion Detectives.

How Is This Workbook Organized?

To make the material easy for your child to find, the child components of the workbook all appear directly after this introduction in Chapters 1 through 12. The material is organized by session, with one chapter typically corresponding to one session. Parent workbook materials appear after all child workbook materials (in Chapters 13–17) and are organized according to the five CLUES skills of treatment.

What About My Role as a Parent in this Treatment?

Whether your child is 7 or 13, you (rather than your child's therapist) are actually the most important support person on your child's detective team. Although your child's therapist will be the one teaching your child the skills, you play a crucial role in helping your child to achieve mastery over these skills and to apply them to deal with strong emotions in all different types of situations. You will learn the same skills your child is learning during the parent sessions and through reviewing the parent chapters of this workbook. As a result, you will be well equipped to identify times when your child can benefit from using Emotion Detective skills (also sometimes referred to as CLUES skills), to coach your child through using these skills, and to reward your child afterward so that it is more likely that he or she will continue to use these skills in the future. Because your child won't learn the skills as well if you don't learn to use them too, it is important that you attend every session of this treatment to the extent possible.

Parent sessions and workbook content will also help you identify whether your own emotions may sometimes get in the way of using the most effective strategies possible to parent your emotional child, resulting in the use of **emotional parenting behaviors**. This program teaches you some strategies for replacing these emotional parenting behaviors with **opposite parenting behaviors** that research has shown to be more effective in helping to manage and reduce your child's level of strong emotions. How you and other adults in your child's life respond to your child's emotions can change the course and intensity of your child's emotional experiences. The parenting strategies you will learn in this program may help you learn to respond to your child's emotions in a way that reduces their intensity and the amount of time they last.

Will My Child and I Have to Do Anything Outside of Treatment Sessions?

The short answer to this question is—yes! Practicing skills in session will only take you and your child so far. Research shows that it is important to practice using skills in all the types of real-world situations where difficult emotions—such as anxiety, sadness, or anger—typically come up. Just because your child learns to use a particular skill in one situation or when experiencing one emotion doesn't necessarily mean your child will automatically know how to apply that skill in a different situation or in response to a very different emotion. The same principle applies to the parenting strategies we cover in this program. You may be able to very effectively use a particular parenting strategy in one situation, with a good response from your child, but struggle to use it effectively in other situations. Your group leaders will ask both you and your child to practice the skills you are learning by completing **home learning assignments** each week. Completing these assignments at home and then reviewing them in session will allow you and your child to receive specific and detailed feedback about what seems to be going well and about how to adjust your use of the skills to make them even more effective.

What Should I Tell My Child About this Treatment?

Many parents experience significant anxiety and anticipation about introducing the idea of treatment to their child. It is important to discuss this program with your child before you begin, but parents often worry that, if they tell their child about the program, their child will feel singled out or will come to believe something is wrong with him or her. When you discuss this treatment with your child, we recommend normalizing your child's struggle with strong emotions by introducing the idea that *everyone* is bothered at times by strong feelings of sadness, anger, anxiety, or fear. You may even wish to discuss a time when you struggled with one of these strong emotions yourself. Emphasize that there is nothing different about or wrong with your child—rather, his or her strong emotions are just causing more trouble than usual right now, so it is time to get some help.

Remember that this program is probably a new and scary experience for your child. Some children may also feel angry about having to participate in the program because they feel they don't have a big problem managing their emotions or because there are many other things they would rather be doing. If your child does resist participating, try not to argue with her or him but do express empathy and understanding of the emotions and thoughts your child is experiencing. Encourage your child to at least attend the first session, and offer a reward for attending. In our experience, most children enjoy the first session of treatment and want to come back.

Treatment is a significant time commitment, and some children and their parents worry that participating in treatment might take time away from schoolwork or other activities that the child enjoys. This may certainly be true—aside from the time you and your child spend attending and getting to and from treatment, you may find that your child is tired when you get home and it is too late to get much schoolwork done. Although this can be frustrating for children and parents alike, it is important to remember that the purpose of this treatment is to develop new skills for ultimately reducing stress and anxiety around schoolwork and for enjoying activities more. Remember that this treatment is temporary, and the sacrifices you and your family make to participate in this treatment will likely reap big rewards in the future.

Any Other Advice You Can Give Me Before Beginning Treatment?

This program requires hard work from both you and your child, but it can also be a fun and rewarding experience. Whenever possible, we encourage you to bring the spirit of the Emotion Detectives program home by encouraging your child to solve mysteries, conduct experiments, and look for clues related to his or her emotions when not in treatment. The more fun and memorable you make these skills, the better able your child will be to understand them, practice them, and apply them to difficult situations. Let's get started!

Unified Protocol
for Transdiagnostic Treatment
of Emotional Disorders
in Children

Welcome to the UP-C and Emotion Detectives!

Hi everyone! Welcome to Emotion Detectives, a special program that will help you learn about emotions like being happy, sad, joyful, angry, surprised, and scared. This program will also help you learn more about how to deal with some of the tough emotions that kids need to handle sometimes.

Everyone has emotions, even tough ones. Emotions are very important to have! But, sometimes, strong or tough emotions can lead us to do some not so helpful things. They may cause us to feel really upset, make us want to miss out on time with friends or family, give us trouble sleeping or eating, lead us to feel like we don't want to do fun things we used to like doing, or even cause us to have big arguments or fights with our friends or family.

In this program, which we call the Unified Protocol for Children (UP-C) or in this workbook, Emotion Detectives, we will work with you to learn new, more helpful ways to deal with some of these tough emotions that you might be having.

During this first session of Emotion Detectives, we are going to start by:

1. Getting to know each other and telling you more about how we are going to help you.

2. Learning about the different parts of an emotion.

3. Learning more about what we do when we are having an emotion and how the things we do when we are sad, angry, or scared can be helpful or not so helpful to us.

Let us start by introducing ourselves. Our names are **Jack** and **Nina** and we are Emotion Detectives. Do you know what detectives do? I bet that if you work together with your therapist, you might be able to figure out some of the really great things we do as detectives. Once we know what a detective does, we can think about how being a detective can help us with our strong emotions.

What do detectives do?

Write down some of your ideas in our list below!
Share your ideas when you finish.

_____

_____

_____

_____

_____

Work together with your parent and your therapist to figure out your **three biggest reasons** for coming to Emotion Detectives. A lot of times, the things that bother us the most are things that make us feel scared, sad, nervous, or mad.

For example, some kids may be here because they are very afraid of dogs, because they worry a lot before they take tests, or because they have a hard time having fun even when they are doing things they used to enjoy. Your biggest problems might be like these, or they might be totally different!

After identifying three "top problems," work with your parent and your therapist to identify a goal that is related to each problem.

For example, if your problem is being very afraid around dogs, your goal might be to pet a dog.

Top Problems:

1. _____

What is my goal?_____

2. _____

What is my goal?_____

3. _____

What is my goal?_____

Now that you have thought a bit about what detectives do and your goals for treatment, we should probably tell you that Emotion Detectives like us aren't just any detectives; we are special detectives who help kids like you figure out how to notice, understand, and deal with tough emotions. To do this, we will teach you to use a whole lot of skills that we call the CLUES skills.

These skills spell out the word CLUES because just like detectives solve mysteries, we will be working together to use our skills to figure out how to deal with tough emotions!

C onsider how I feel

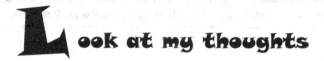

L ook at my thoughts

U se Detective Thinking & Problem Solving

E xperience my Emotions

S tay healthy and happy!

Figure 1.1

Clues Skills

We all do different things when we are having an emotion. Work with your therapist to try to think of some helpful and less helpful things we can do when we have strong emotions like being scared, worried, sad, or angry.

We have given you an example to get you started!

Helpful	Less Helpful
I am feeling sad one day so I go to the playground with my friends because I know I'll have more fun with them and feel better.	I am feeling sad one day so I stay home and take a nap. I wake up and feel even more sad and bored because I didn't do anything fun today!

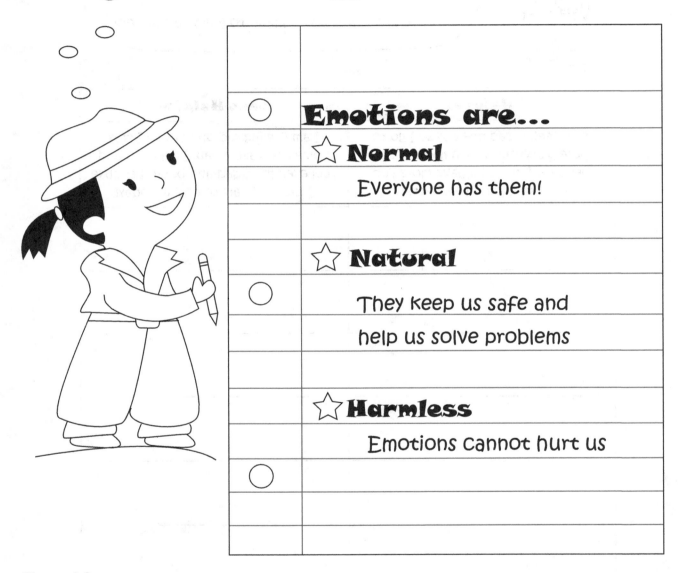

Figure 1.2

Normal, Natural, & Harmless

Worksheet 1.4: My Emotions at Home

You have learned a lot about different emotions so far. Use this worksheet at home to check off which days you feel the emotions listed over the next week. This way, we can build our Emotion Detective skill of noticing our emotions.

Anger	Fear	Surprise	Happiness	Sadness
☐ Monday	☐ Monday	☐ Monday	☐ Monday	☐ Monday
☐ Tuesday	☐ Tuesday	☐ Tuesday	☐ Tuesday	☐ Tuesday
☐ Wednesday	☐ Wednesday	☐ Wednesday	☐ Wednesday	☐ Wednesday
☐ Thursday	☐ Thursday	☐ Thursday	☐ Thursday	☐ Thursday
☐ Friday	☐ Friday	☐ Friday	☐ Friday	☐ Friday
☐ Saturday	☐ Saturday	☐ Saturday	☐ Saturday	☐ Saturday
☐ Sunday	☐ Sunday	☐ Sunday	☐ Sunday	☐ Sunday

Using one strong emotion you felt this week, fill in the section below.

The emotion I chose to write about is: _____

This is what happened: _____

The emotional behavior (what the emotion made me want to do) was: _____
_____

During this session we will:

1. Talk about all the different emotions we have.

2. Learn that emotions are normal, natural, and harmless.

3. Learn about the three parts of an emotion.

4. Learn how the parts of our emotions work together to lead to less helpful actions sometimes.

5. Talk about rewards for new and brave behaviors.

Session 2

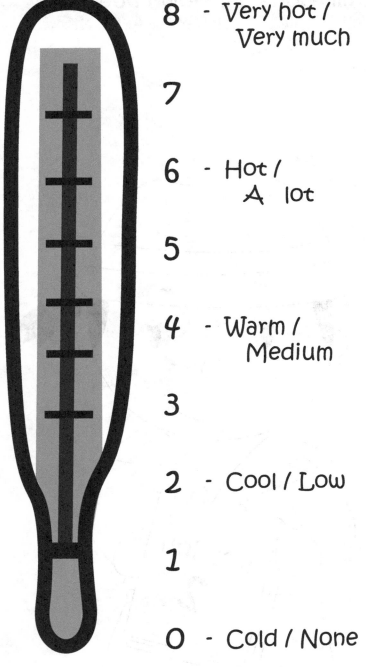

8 - Very hot /
    Very much

7

6 - Hot /
    A lot

5

4 - Warm /
    Medium

3

2 - Cool / Low

1

0 - Cold / None

Jack back with you again!

To get us started, we will be using this emotion thermometer just like a real thermometer! With a real thermometer, the temperature gets hotter or higher when your fever is stronger and lower when your body is cooler. Just like that, as our emotions get stronger, the number on the emotion thermometer goes up. Work with your therapist to figure out what kinds of things cause you to feel strong emotions!

We might feel stronger emotions at different times or when we have different thoughts. When Nina is about to go on a roller coaster, she feels scared at a 4. When I go on a roller coaster, I feel scared at a 0, but I feel scared at a 4 when I see a bumble bee!

Figure 2.1

The Emotion Thermometer

Consider Your Thoughts, Feelings, and Behaviors

After you learn about the parts of an emotion, you and your therapist should fill this out during session focusing on one strong emotion you had recently!

What happened? (Trigger)

_____

_____

_____

1. What was I thinking about? (Thoughts)

_____

_____

_____

2. What was I feeling in my body? (Body Clues)

_____

_____

_____

3. What did I do (or want to do)? (Behaviors)

_____

_____

_____

Thoughts

Body Clues

Behaviors

A very important part of an emotion is the behavior part, or what we do when we have a strong emotion. Two common things we do when we have strong emotions are **avoiding** (staying away from something that makes us feel sad, afraid, or worried) and behaviors like yelling or fighting when we feel upset or angry. We call these things we do **emotional behaviors**.

Jack gets scared about meeting new people sometimes. If he never goes to any parties because it makes him feel scared, what would happen? Nina gets angry when her parents want her to do her homework. How do you think her parents would react if Nina yelled and slammed the door at homework time each night?

Emotional behaviors like avoiding or yelling MAY make us feel better right now, but they make us feel worse or cause more problems for us later on.

Figure 2.2

Cycle of Emotions and Behaviors

Special activities or rewards for new and brave behavior

Nina here! Great job this week thinking about your emotions. We know that doing new and brave behaviors can be hard for kids. Getting rewards can sometimes make doing hard stuff easier for us!

Work with your parents to come up with some ideas for rewards to increase new and brave behaviors. Your therapist can help too! Rewards might include **special activities** like playing your favorite board game, or going to a movie with your parent. Rewards could also include ~~treats~~ like spending time with a friend you don't get to see much, or even going out for a scoop of ice cream!

Make sure you come up with a range of ideas, some smaller rewards (like getting stickers) and some bigger ones (going to a movie or get-ting to pick what you have for dinner).

Rewards for things that are a little bit hard to do:

_____

_____

_____

Rewards for things that are harder to do:

_____

_____

_____

Rewards for things that are really hard to do:

_____

_____

_____

Form 2.1: Solving the Mystery of Our Emotions: Before, During, and After

Each week, you will be asked to solve the mystery of **at least** one strong emotion by writing down the Before, During, and **A**fter of your response to that strong emotion. Solving this mystery is the first step to learning new things that can help when we feel these strong emotions. By keeping track of at least one emotion each week and referring back to them later, you can see how what you think, feel, or do can help you uncover the mystery of your emotions.

| What happened Before? (What was the trigger?) | What happened During? | | What happened After? (What happened right away? What happened later?) |
	Thoughts	Body Clues	Behaviors	
Week 2:				
Week 3:				
Week 4:				
Week 5:				

What happened **Before?** (What was the trigger?)	What happened **During?**		What happened **After?** (What happened right away? What happened later?)
	Thoughts	Body Clues	Behaviors	
Week 6:				
Week 7:				
Week 8:				
Week 9:				
Week 10:				

What happened Before? (What was the trigger?)	What happened During?		Behaviors	What happened After? (What happened right away? What happened later?)
	Thoughts	Body Clues		
Week 11:				
Week 12:				
Week 13:				
Week 14:				
Week 15:				

During this session we will:

1. Learn about acting opposite to emotional behaviors that aren't helping us.

2. Talk about what a science experiment is and how to do one to help learn more about acting opposite.

3. Learn about what activities we do to act opposite when we feel sad.

4. Do an experiment this week at home to see how we feel when we do different fun activities.

Worksheet 3.1: Acting Opposite

In session, your therapist may tell you that our emotions can become tough to deal with or make us want to do things to make them go away, even if those things we do don't really help us in the long run.

When we notice that our emotions might be making us want to act in less helpful ways, we can try doing the **opposite**. Doing the opposite of what our strong emotions want us to do can be hard, but can make things easier later on!

Work with your therapist to list some of the emotions you have had lately, what they make you want to do, and what doing the opposite would be. We have filled out the first one for you!

Emotion	What it makes you want to do	Doing the opposite
Anger	Yell and cry when my mom tells me to stop playing videogames, even though I might get in trouble for it.	Take a deep breath and give myself a minute to calm down before I respond. This way, I don't get in trouble!

Your therapist might have told you a little about **science experiments**. They are one of our favorite things to do as Emotion Detectives because they help us test out the best ways to deal with tough emotions!

We are going to do a science experiment to figure out how doing the opposite of what sad feelings make us want to do might change our emotions. What do sad feelings make us want to do? What is the opposite of that?

Write down your ideas for how to do a science experiment when feeling sad!

1. **Start with a question**
   (What else can I do after school when I feel sad?)
   _____
   _____

2. **Make a guess**
   (Maybe try kicking a ball outside)
   _____
   _____

3. **Try out experiment**
   (I'm going to try it for 10 minutes)
   _____
   _____

4. **Watch how it goes**
   (I actually do feel a little better)
   _____
   _____

5. **Try my experiment again!**
   (I'll play for 15 minutes tomorrow. Maybe my sister can play too)
   _____
   _____

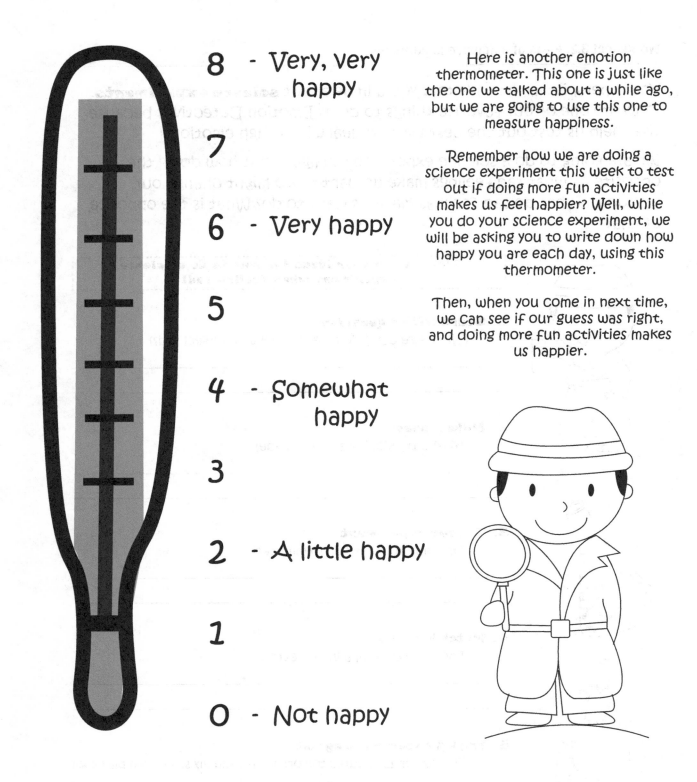

8 - Very, very happy

7

6 - Very happy

5

4 - Somewhat happy

3

2 - A little happy

1

0 - Not happy

Here is another emotion thermometer. This one is just like the one we talked about a while ago, but we are going to use this one to measure happiness.

Remember how we are doing a science experiment this week to test out if doing more fun activities makes us feel happier? Well, while you do your science experiment, we will be asking you to write down how happy you are each day, using this thermometer.

Then, when you come in next time, we can see if our guess was right, and doing more fun activities makes us happier.

Figure 3.1

The Emotion Thermometer for Happy

Here is an example of an Emotion and Activity Diary that Nina has filled out for one week. Use this example to help you fill out **your own** Emotion and Activity Diary on Worksheet 3.5.

Day of the Week	Emotion Rating	Activities Completed	Notes
Monday	4	Tried out for a play at school and ate lunch with friends	Great day
Tuesday	2	Skipped choir to go home early after school	Not as great
Wednesday	3	Didn't do anything after school	Boring day, not much to do
Thursday	2	Went home and cried after school	Feeling really down, only got a small part in the school play
Friday	2	Stayed home and watched TV	Felt bored
Saturday	2	Stayed home and watched more TV	Really bored
Sunday	2	Went to the mall with mom, went home and napped	The mall was more fun than I thought it would be

What did you notice about Nina's feelings and activities?_____

Here's a clue: What we **do** or **don't do** can affect our emotions or moods!

Figure 3.2

Nina's Emotion and Activity Diary

Worksheet 3.3: List of Activities

At the bottom of this worksheet is a list of activities (like things to do, places to go, and things to learn) you can try out when you are feeling down or sad. Remember that when we do things we enjoy, we usually begin to feel happier!

Remember the four types of activities you learned about:

Helping Others: doing something to help others

Learning New Things: doing something to learn a skill, working toward being an expert

Doing Things with People: doing something fun with friends or family members

Moving Our Bodies: getting up and doing some activity like playing a game

Try to choose activities from this list or come up with your own to see how changing your activity affects your emotions.

Which of the categories above do these activities fall into?

Visiting the Aquarium
Doing an Arts and crafts project
Doing Martial Arts
Going to the Park
Playing Baseball
Playing Basketball
Going to the Beach
Going to a Museum
Doing Choir
Joining a Cooking Class
Doing Volunteer Work
Playing on the Computer
Going to a Concert
Joining a Church/
Youth Group
Joining a Dance Class
Dancing to a Favorite Song

Playing Field Hockey
Watching Movies
Learning a Foreign Language
Taking Golf Lessons
Playing Laser Tag
Going Shopping
Doing Yoga
Playing Hockey Ice/Roller
Skating
Playing Instruments
Knitting/Sewing Playing
Lacrosse
Biking Babysitting
Reading a good book
Running Sailing/Boating
Scrapbooking Skateboarding
Singing at the top of
your lungs

Playing Football
Baking Cookies
Taking Pictures
Learning Sign Language
Playing Soccer
Playing Volleyball
Swimming
Walking your dog Writing
Hiking
Going to the Zoo
Playing Tennis
Doing Yard Work
Think of your own and list here!

_____

_____

_____

Use this chart to write a list of activities. If you have trouble thinking of ideas, you can use your "List of Activities" worksheet. Try to pick things that will make you feel good, and also include things that are easy to do, and you can do without needing to plan too much!

	Activity
1	
2	
3	
4	
5	
6	
7	
8	
9	
10	

This week, you try to make your own Emotion and Activity Diary just like Nina did. Remember to try to notice if your mood is better on the days you do more fun stuff!

Day of the Week	Emotion Rating	Activities Completed	Notes

What did you notice about your activities and emotions?

_____

0 1 2 3 4 5 6 7 8

Form 3.1: Acting Opposite Plans

Session 1	Session 2	Session 3	Session 4	Session 5
Session 6	Session 7	Session 8	Session 9	Session 10
Session 11	Session 12	Session 13	Session 14	Session 15

During this session we will:

1. Learn what body clues are and when they happen.

2. Learn a skill called body scanning and use it to help us find our body clues.

3. Practice making body clues happen on purpose!

Session 4

Figure 4.1

What Are Body Clues?

Hi again! Jack here. Today we are going to work together to become **body detectives**. Now that we have learned what body clues are, we are ready to get to work!

Body detectives are super-cool Emotion Detectives who are really good at knowing what body clues they feel when they are having different emotions! Work with your therapist to think of some emotions like the ones listed here and if those emotions make you feel any of these common body clues. Then, write down which body clues you have the most at the bottom of this figure!

Emotion	Body Clues
Happiness	Feel like smiling, feel warm inside, heart beating fast
Fear	Feel dizzy, heart beating fast, face feels hot, feel sweaty, muscles feel tight or hot, shaking, mouth feeling dry, out of breath
Sadness	Feel heavy, chest feels tight, feel like crying, shaking, throat feels tight, eyes hurt, feel tired, feel like moving slowly
Anger	Face feels hot, muscles feel tight and hot, mouth feels dry, hands and feet feel tight, hot or shaky, throat feels tight, chest feels tight, feel like yelling, screaming
Anxiety	Brain feels full, heart beating fast, face feels hot, muscles feel tight, feel like yelling, screaming, stomach hurts or head hurts, feel nauseous
Which body clue do you have the most?	

Figure 4.2

Becoming a Body Detective

Worksheet 4.1: Finding Your Body Clues

Let's practice being body detectives! Using a big piece of paper from your therapist or the outline below, try to write down the body clues you have had for some emotions.

Some kids find it helpful to use different colors for different emotions (for example, red for anger, blue for sadness, yellow for happiness, and green for fear).

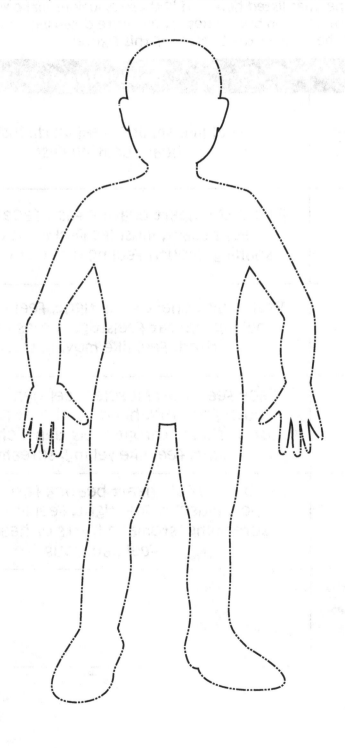

OK everyone! The next step to becoming really great body detectives is learning how to body scan. Body scanning is a special activity you will do now with your therapist to find any body clues you might be having!

Body scanning is very helpful because we can use it anytime and it can help us notice any body clues we are having, as well as watch what happens to our body clues as time passes.

Jack's Steps to Body Scanning

1 Close your eyes. Starting at the tip-top of your head, slowly move down your body. **Notice** any parts of your body that feel tight and uncomfortable. Make sure you move down all the way to your toes.

2 As you notice each body clue, rate how strong each one is on a 0-8 scale.

3 **Say something** to yourself about what each body clue feels like.

4 **Experience** each body clue by sticking with the feeling, even if it is uncomfortable. Notice how your body clues change over time.

5 After you have practiced experiencing your body clues, rate again how strong each one is.

What do you notice?

Figure 4.3

How to Body Scan!

Form 4.1: Monitoring How My Body Feels

As you practice science experiments with your therapist in session, use this chart to write down the different experiments you try (exercises), the body clues you feel (physical sensations), how strong the body clues feel on our emotion thermometer (0–8), and anything else you notice during the experiment (notes).

Rating Scale:

	0	1	2	3	4	5	6	7	8
	None		A Little		Medium		Strong		Very Strong

Experiment	Body Clues	How strong are your body clues? (0–8)	Notes (e.g., thoughts, emotions, behaviors?)

Worksheet 4.2: Finding Your Body Clues at Home

This week, work with your parents to practice scanning for body clues at home by doing one of our experiments that made you feel the strongest body clues.

This week, I will try_____.

Write down the body clues you had on the outline below!

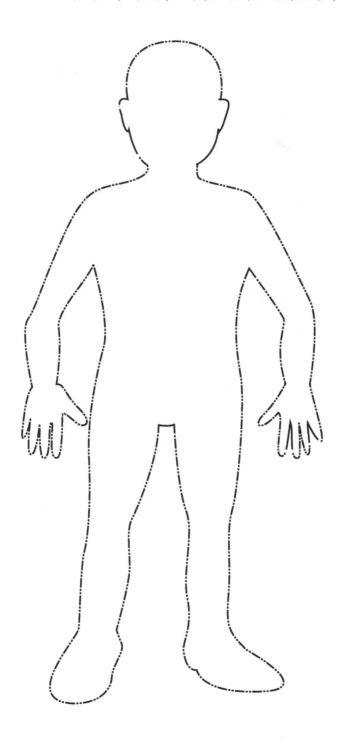

During this session we will:

1. Learn what it means to be a flexible thinker.

2. Learn about something we all do: fall into thinking traps!

3. Meet some **new detectives** who also fall into thinking traps sometimes!

Worksheet 5.1: What Are Snap Judgments?

There is usually more than one way to understand the things going on around us.

Work with your therapist to think about some things that happened to Jack. Try to decide what his first thought was in this situation and if there is another thought that he could have in this same situation!

Jack walks by a group of kids laughing. He thinks that they must be making fun of him.

First thought: _____

_____

Another thought: _____

_____

Jack waves to his friend across the hallway, but his friend doesn't wave back. He thinks his friend must be angry at him.

First thought: _____

_____

Another thought: _____

_____

Jack strikes out during a baseball game. He thinks he must be a terrible player.

First thought: _____

_____

Another thought: _____

_____

Jack's first thought in these situations is called his **snap judgment** because it is the first thing he thinks right away.

Snap judgments help us figure out things that are happening to us really quickly so that our brains don't have to work so hard. However, when we are feeling strong emotions, sometimes our brains focus first on *unhelpful things* that make us feel even stronger emotions!

We call these unhelpful things that our minds get stuck on **thinking traps.** Your therapist will tell you about the thinking traps that Emotion Detectives might fall into. Getting stuck in these traps can make even the best Emotion Detectives feel anxious or down!

On this page, we (Jack and Nina) have made up nicknames for ourselves and our Emotion Detective friends so that you know which thinking traps we tend to get stuck in!

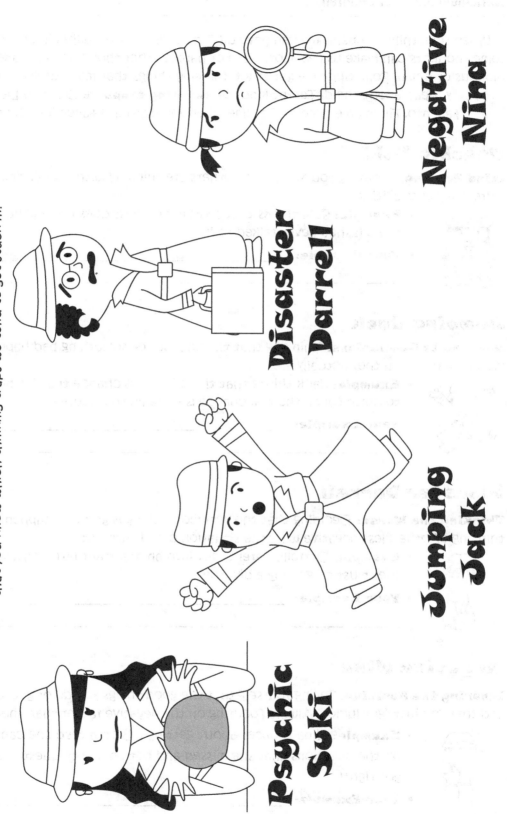

Psychic Suki

Jumping Jack

Disaster Darrell

Negative Nina

Figure 5.1

Thinking Traps and Emotion Detectives

When something happens, we can have different types of thoughts in our minds. While some thoughts can make us feel more calm or happy, other thoughts can make us feel more anxious or down. Sometimes we get stuck thinking things that make us feel anxious, down, or angry. Read about the different kinds of **thinking traps** we Emotion Detectives can fall into. Fill in an example of a time when you may have fallen into each trap.

Psychic Suki

Mind Reading: Believing you know what others are thinking without figuring out other, more likely possibilities.

- **Example:** Suki thinks that a girl in her class does not like her, even though she's never talked to her.
- **Your Example:** _____
  _____

Jumping Jack

Jumping to Conclusions: Thinking that the chances of something bad happening are much greater than they actually are.

- **Example:** Jack thinks that there is a 90% chance that his plane is going to crash (when the real chance is more like 0.00002%).
- **Your Example:** _____
  _____

Disaster Darrell

Thinking the Worst: Deciding that the very worst thing is going to happen, without thinking of other, less negative ways the situation could turn out.

- **Example:** Darrell's parents got into an argument last night, so he thinks they must be getting a divorce.
- **Your Example:** _____
  _____

Negative Nina

Ignoring the Positive: Telling yourself that the good things you do or get "don't count" and that you just "got lucky." Always focusing on the negative rather than the positive.

- **Example:** Nina is upset about getting a B on a test; she can only focus on the questions that she missed and not on all the questions that she got right!
- **Your Example:** _____
  _____

Let's practice identifying thinking traps. Once we are better able to understand which thoughts lead to thinking traps, we will get better and better at noticing our own thinking traps. Work with your therapist to practice matching each emotional thought to the thinking trap the Emotion Detective is falling into!

Psychic Suki
Mind Reading

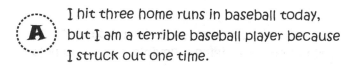

A — I hit three home runs in baseball today, but I am a terrible baseball player because I struck out one time.

Jumping Jack
Jumping to Conclusions

B — Oh no! There are dark clouds outside. There is definitely going to be a storm.

Disaster Darrell
Thinking the Worst

C — My friend must be mad at me because she is making an angry face when I see her in the hallway at school.

Negative Nina
Ignoring the Positive

D — I got a C on my math test. I am definitely going to fail out of school and end up homeless.

Let's think about how Jack could be a flexible thinker using the trap you and your therapist figured out that he fell into on **Worksheet 5.3.** As a reminder, here is Jack's thinking trap:

"Oh no! There are dark clouds outside. There is definitely going to be a big storm."

Work with your therapist to write down how Jack can use the three steps to being a flexible thinker to help him climb out of his thinking trap.

Jack's Steps to Being a Flexible Thinker

1. Identify the thinking trap! Which thinking trap is Jack stuck in?

_____

_____

2. What else might be true?

_____

_____

_____

3. Detective Thinking

Next week, we will learn how to do this last step of flexible thinking to help Jack look for clues that will tell him whether his thinking trap thought is true or not.

This week, work with your parents to figure out which thinking trap you are falling into when you are having a strong emotion like feeling scared, sad, anxious, or angry. Then, write down your thought in its thinking trap box below! Try to fill in at least three boxes this week. It's okay if you get stuck in one kind of thinking trap more than others.

Psychic Suki

1. _____
2. _____
3. _____

Jumping Jack

1. _____
2. _____
3. _____

Disaster Darrell

1. _____
2. _____
3. _____

Negative Nina

1. _____
2. _____
3. _____

During this session we will:

1. Play a mystery game that will help teach us a new skill called **Detective Thinking**, which helps Emotion Detectives think in more flexible ways.

2. Practice using Detective Thinking to help climb out of thinking traps and be a more flexible thinker!

Session 6

Emotion Detectives like Nina and Jack are really good at solving mysteries, especially those that have to do with getting out of **thinking traps**.

To show you how to do this, let's first practice solving an easier mystery and save the tougher thinking trap work for later.

Work with your therapist to write down the *type of mystery* you are going to practice solving. Then jot down the clues you find while solving that mystery. When you are done, write down your best guess about the answer to your mystery question.

It is MUCH easier to solve a mystery when you use clues to help you figure it out!

The mystery I am going to try to solve is:

CLUES:

1. _____

_____

2. _____

_____

3. _____

_____

4. _____

_____

I think the answer to the mystery is:

Worksheet 6.2: U for Children

You have been talking about what a thinking trap is with your therapist. Emotion Detectives can help themselves deal with their thinking traps using mystery-solving skills!

Work with your therapist to go over the steps of Detective Thinking: Stop, Slow, and Go!

Your therapist might have you use information from last week's home learning assignment to practice the steps together.

Steps		Answers
	What is the situation?	
	What is the thought?	
Best guess about what is happening	How likely is it to happen? (0–100%)	
	What is the thinking trap?	
	What's happened in the past? Have I coped with this situation before?	
Clues	Am I 100% sure that my emotional thought is true?	
	What else could be true?	
	Is there anything good about this situation?	
	If my emotional thought is true, can I cope with it?	
Check your best guess	How likely is it to happen? (0–100%)	
What are my coping thoughts?		

Worksheet 6.3: Detective Thinking Practice

Let's practice solving some more mysteries! Maybe you and your therapist can work together to help some of our Emotion Detectives here climb out of their thinking traps by gathering clues that help them become more flexible thinkers.

Darrell: "I got in a fight with my best friend on the way here. I don't even know what it was about now. I can't believe it! We'll probably never talk to each other again! And if we stop talking, I won't be able to hang out with all our other friends! I started the Detective Thinking steps. Can you help me finish?"

Steps		Answers
What is the situation?		I got in a fight with my friend.
What is the thought?		We will probably never talk again and I will lose all the friends we have in common!
Best guess about what is happening	How likely is it to happen? (0–100%)	90% because it seems like it is totally true since I feel so sad about it.
Clues	What is Darrell's thinking trap?	Thinking the worst (we call that Disaster Darrell since this happens to Darrell a lot)
	What's happened in the past? Have I coped with this situation before?	I've been in arguments with this friend many times. We usually stay mad for a few hours and then someone apologizes and everything is OK.
	Is Darrell 100% sure that his emotional thought is true?	I guess not... This isn't the first time this has happened and I have never lost friends like that
	What else could be true?	
	Is there anything good about this situation?	
	If Darrell's emotional thought is true, can he cope with it?	
Check your best guess	How likely is it to happen? (0–100%)	
What are Darrell's coping thoughts?		

Great job! Can you help Jack with his thinking trap too? Jack filled in some of the answers for you. Can you help him finish gathering clues to help him get out of his thinking trap?

Jack: "My mom was 10 minutes late picking me up from soccer practice. I was sure that she had been in an accident and was probably hurt. I started Detective Thinking and gathering clues. Can you help me get out of my thinking trap?"

Steps		Answers
What is the situation?		Mom is 10 minutes late.
What is the thought?		Mom got in an accident and was probably hurt.
Best guess about what is happening	How likely is it to happen? (0–100%)	80% because I really feel like it happened!
Clues	What is Jack's thinking trap?	Jumping to Conclusions (we call this one Jumping Jack for short since Jack falls into it a lot)
	What's happened in the past? Have I coped with this situation before?	She's been late before because there was traffic or my sister took a long time getting ready to leave school.
	Is Jack 100% sure that his emotional thought is true?	I guess not.... She has been late before and she was not hurt or anything.
	What else could be true?	
	Is there anything good about this situation?	
	If Jack's emotional thought is true, can he cope with it?	
Check your best guess	How likely is it to happen? (0–100%)	
What are Jack's coping thoughts?		

49

Now that you know all the steps of **Detective Thinking**, work with your therapist to review when the best times are to use this skill! When these types of things come up during the week, you can practice using Detective Thinking with your parents or on your own.

★ When you're starting a new school year and you don't know if your teacher will be nice, or your teacher looks mad and you don't know why.

★ When you feel angry or sad at school because kids or your teacher say something you don't like.

★ When you are studying or doing homework and don't know how you'll ever finish everything.

★ When you're about to take a test or about to get a test back and you're not sure how you did.

★ When you're angry because you think your grade on a test is unfair.

★ When you're going to meet new kids at a party or event.

★ When somebody at a party or event makes you feel left out.

★ When you're invited to something fun but you feel too down to go.

★ When you are doing something new for the first time.

★ When you need to be near something or do something that feels scary, like be by a dog if you are afraid of dogs or go on an elevator if you are afraid of elevators.

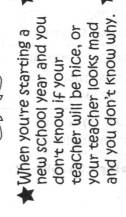

Figure 6.1

When to Use Detective Thinking

This week, work with your parents or on your own to notice one time when you fall into a thinking trap.

Remember, thinking traps are thoughts that happen really fast and often lead to strong emotions like being anxious, sad, scared, or angry. When we get stuck in a thinking trap, it is hard to have any other thoughts about a situation that might calm us down.

The Detective Thinking steps below can help us deal with our thinking traps well and learn to be even more flexible thinkers!

★ What is the situation? _____

_____

★ What is the thought? _____

_____

Best guess about what is happening	**Clues**
How likely is it to happen? (0–100%) _____	★ What is the thinking trap? _____ ★ What's happened in the past? Have I coped with this situation before? _____ _____ ★ Am I 100% sure that emotional thought is true? _____ ★ What else could be true? _____ _____ ★ Is there anything good about this situation? _____ _____ ★ If my emotional thought is true, can I cope with it? _____

Check your best guess	**What are my coping thoughts?**
How likely is it to happen? (0–100%) _____	_____ _____ _____

During this session we will:

1. Learn a new skill called **Problem Solving** by playing a game together.

2. Practice using Problem Solving to help get unstuck when we are in tough situations!

3. Learn how to use Problem Solving with other people, like friends or family.

Problem Solving is another type of Emotion Detective skill you can use to help you get out of situations where you may have trouble coming up with what to DO (like if you feel like you don't have enough time to do your homework or if you had a fight with your parents). Here are some steps for knowing how to be a good problem solver!

Nina's Steps to Problem Solving

1 **Define the problem**
What you decide the problem is will affect the solutions you choose. Keep it simple when writing down your problem!

- **Example:** "I want to do better in math, but I am not sure what to do that can help."

- **Example:** "I am scared to go to a birthday party on Saturday night because I may not know anyone there."

2 **Brainstorm solutions**
Come up a few solutions or things you could do that would help. Try not to decide which are good or bad solutions yet. Just come up with ideas that could help.
Always come up with at least one ~~goofy~~ solution to get your mind thinking flexibly!

3 **List the pros and cons for each solution**
Try to come up with at least one good thing and one bad thing about each of the possible solutions or ideas that you came up with.

4 **Pick a solution and try it out**
Based on your pros and cons list, pick one idea to try out. Be specific about how and when you will put your solution into place.

5 **If needed, go through the Problem Solving steps again**
If the first solution you try doesn't work, you can either try a second one or go back to step one and try again. It may help to change the way you describe the problem or to think of other solutions.

Figure 7.1

Problem Solving Steps

We Emotion Detectives have lots of different skills that help us solve the mysteries of our emotions.

Today, we are going to work on our Problem Solving steps together.

Let's start out by practicing solving an easier problem and save the tougher Problem Solving work for later today.

① Define the problem

Getting a toy across the room without using your hands!

② Brainstorm solutions

1. _____
2. _____
3. _____
4. _____
5. _____

③ List the pros and cons for each solution

Solutions	Pros	Cons
1.		
2.		
3.		
4.		
5.		

④ Pick a solution and try it out!

My solution is:

Now that you know a bit about Problem Solving, can you help Jack solve a problem he has been having? Jack started filling in the Problem Solving steps but needs some help finishing:

Jack: "I really like playing videogames, but right now I'm not allowed to. I missed a couple days of school last week, and I'm still behind on my homework. My mom said I can't play until my grades in school are better. But, sometimes I feel really down and I don't want to go to school, do my homework, or do anything but play video games!"

---

1 Define the problem

Jack wants to play videogames but he isn't allowed to until his grades get better.

2 Brainstorm solutions

1. I could try to play videogames when my parents aren't home.

2. I could work hard in school and get a better grade on my next test.

3. I could go over to Suki's house to play games there.

4. _____

Any other ideas?

5. _____

3 List the pros and cons for each solution

Solutions	Pros	Cons
1.	If I don't get caught then I can play without working on my grades.	I could get caught and get in more trouble.
2.	I could earn my games back the right way!	Studying for tests is really hard when I feel down.
3.	I would get to play videogames at Suki's house.	My mom might get mad that I'm playing videogames at someone else's house.
4.		
5.		

4 Pick a solution and try it out!

Jack's solution should be:

Can you also help Nina solve a problem? Lots of kids sometimes have problems with other kids or family members. Work with your therapist to try to help Nina solve her problem.

Nina: "Well, I've been feeling really angry at my best friend lately. Last weekend she had a party and didn't invite me! I cried a lot on Saturday when I found out. I was really angry and sad! I saw her at school on Monday and I was so mad that I didn't even look at her all day!"

---

① Define the problem

---

② Brainstorm solutions

1. _____
2. _____
3. _____
4. _____
5. _____

---

③ List the pros and cons for each solution

What are some good & bad things about these solutions?

Solutions	Pros	Cons
1.	_____	_____
2.	_____	_____
3.	_____	_____
4.	_____	_____
5.	_____	_____

---

④ Pick a solution and try it out!

Nina's solution should be:

Maybe we can all work together to try to help you solve a problem that you might be having!

Some problems have to do with school, friends, parents, or not knowing how to go about doing something.

See if you or your therapist can come up with a problem to practice solving together!

① Define the problem

② Brainstorm solutions

1. _____
2. _____
3. _____
4. _____
5. _____

③ List the pros and cons for each solution

Solutions	Pros	Cons
1.	_____	_____
2.	_____	_____
3.	_____	_____
4.	_____	_____
5.	_____	_____

④ Pick a solution and try it out!

My solution is:

Worksheet 7.3: Problem Solving at Home with Others

Today we worked together to solve a silly problem, helped Jack and Nina solve a couple of their own problems about school and friends, and talked about some other problems we might have to solve.

This week, work with your parents or on your own using the steps below to solve a problem you might be having with friends, family, or other kids.

This might be something like feeling left out at school, a teacher saying something that upsets you, your brother or sister annoying you, or arguing with your parents.

Define the problem

The problem is... _____

_____

_____

List the pros and cons for each solution

Brainstorm solutions

	Pros	Cons
1. _____	_____	_____
2. _____	_____	_____
3. _____	_____	_____
4. _____	_____	_____
5. _____	_____	_____

Pick a solution and try it out!

My solution is... _____

_____

_____

 Remember... if needed, go through your Problem Solving steps again!

During this session we will:

1. Use a new Emotion Detective skill to **experience our emotions** while learning three present-moment awareness steps.

2. Practice these **present-moment awareness** steps using our five senses.

3. Learn about and practice **nonjudgmental awareness**, or NJA, another type of awareness we use to help us become experts at experiencing our emotions.

A new Emotion Detective skill we will be learning today is called *experiencing our emotions*. Today we will experience our emotions by focusing our attention on what is going on right now using something we call **present-moment awareness**.

Present-moment awareness has three important steps: Notice things, Say something about things to ourselves, and Experience things in the here and now. Today, we are going to practice using these three steps by doing some fun activities together!

★**Notice it**

Use your five senses (sight, smell, taste, touch, hearing) to see what is going on inside your body and around you. Focus only on the things you notice right now!

★**Say something about it**

Talk to yourself or write down what you noticed.

★**Experience it**

Try to keep your attention focused on the "here and now" for as long as you can; look more, listen more, and notice the things you feel inside of you.

Remember: When you notice a distracting thought or judgment, gently bring yourself back to the present moment.

Figure 8.1

Notice It, Say Something about It, Experience It

Worksheet 8.1: Practicing My Awareness Steps

Work with your therapist to practice noticing, saying
something about, and experiencing what is going on in your
body and around you right now!

First, listen to how your therapist tells you to try this and then
fill in the boxes below.

Notice it

Say something about it

Experience it

Worksheet 8.2: Being Aware with My Five Senses

Let's work together to use the three steps for present-moment awareness—Notice it, Say something about it, and Experience it—while playing the five senses game. During this game, we will work together to use all five senses—seeing, hearing, smelling, tasting, and touching—to pay really close attention to different things. Later, we will work on using this same skill to pay attention to our tough emotions!

What's Around You
• Notice it
_____
_____
• Say something about it
_____
_____
• Experience it
_____
_____

Candy Exercise
• Notice it
_____
_____
• Say something about it
_____
_____
• Experience it
_____
_____

Pebble Exercise
• Notice it
_____
_____
• Say something about it
_____
_____
• Experience it
_____
_____

Play-Doh Exercise
• Notice it
_____
_____
• Say something about it
_____
_____
• Experience it
_____
_____

Work with your therapist to practice present-moment awareness using the five senses game. Here are a few ways you can play this game.

What's around you?

Look around you. Let your eyes be relaxed, not looking for something, or at somewhere because you need to go there. Just look to see what is around you. Let your thoughts slow down as you notice what you see.

Start with the big picture: tables, chairs, walls, pictures, doors. Then begin to take in smaller details: you own hands, fingers, what you're touching. Differing shades of color and light. Maybe one wall of the room you're in right now is in shadow, and another is in full light. Use your other senses, too: do the lights make a buzzing sound, are there cars to be heard passing by? People walking? Notice it with your senses, your eyes and ears. Now let's focus on what you have/are doing right in front of you. Notice it and say something about it to yourself.

Candy Exercise

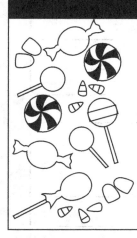

You are an alien, from a planet far, far away. Your first day on Earth, you find some candies in a dish. You have never seen candy before. Pick up one of the candies in the dish. Just notice the candy, looking at it carefully as if you had never seen one before. Feel the candy between your fingers and notice its colors. Use your senses of touch and hearing and sight to notice the candy even better. Be aware of any thoughts you might be having about the candy, even if you don't like this candy. Now, re-focus on the candy and lift it to your nose and smell it for a while. Finally, you are going to use your sense of taste by bringing the candy to your lips, being aware of your arm moving your hand to bring it to your mouth and even your mouth and brain feeling excited about eating it. Take the candy into your mouth and chew it slowly, experiencing the actual taste of the candy. Hold it in your mouth. Pay close attention as you swallow it and it goes down your throat. When you are ready, pick up the second candy and repeat this process again on your own, as if it is now the first candy you have ever seen.

Play-Doh Exercise

Hold and look at a ball of Play-Doh without squeezing it. Notice any feelings like wanting to play with the Play-Doh. Then, describe what you notice about the Play-Doh using your senses. Finally, try making something out of the Play-Doh.

Pebble Exercise

Your therapist will give you a few stones or pebbles to use for this one. Close your eyes and pick up one of the pebbles or stones. While your eyes are closed, use your other senses to try to notice things about the pebble or stone you picked. Tell to yourself any things about the stones that you notice. After a few minutes, and with your eyes still closed, place your pebbles or stones back in the pile with the other ones. With your eyes open and using your other senses, try to find which pebble was yours.

Figure 8.2

Present-Moment Awareness Activities

Worksheet 8.3: Awareness Practice at Home

This week, try to do one awareness activity at home, either with your parents or on your own. It can be using your present-moment awareness skill to play the five senses game, or using nonjudgmental awareness when you are having a tough emotion like feeling anxious, sad, scared, or angry. Fill in the three steps on this worksheet as you practice noticing it, saying something about it, and experiencing this Emotion Detective skill at home!

A good time to practice your awareness steps might be:

_____

Notice it

_____

_____

_____

Say something about it

_____

_____

_____

_____

Experience it

_____

_____

_____

_____

During this session we will:

1. Review Emotion Detective skills learned so far.

2. Remind ourselves what science experiments are and practice one in session.

3. Learn about using science experiments to face our fears and other strong emotions.

4. Practice using our noticing, describing, and experiencing steps during science experiments.

You have already learned a lot of Emotion Detective skills in this program! Since you're becoming such a good Emotion Detective, Jack, Suki, Darrell, and Nina could use your help.

Can you help them figure out which Emotion Detective skill they should use in each of the situations below?

You can use the skills bank at the bottom of the page to help decide what skill they should use.

Situation	Skill Used
Jack is about to make a presentation in class and his heart is beating really fast.	
Suki was home sick from school today and has a test tomorrow. She missed some of the material and needs to figure out what to do.	
Darrell is feeling pretty down today. His mom has work to do so he has just been sitting around, which is making him feel more bored and sad.	
Nina is trying to play baseball but she keeps thinking about how mad she is about an argument she had with her parents and can't focus on the game.	
Suki's best friend has a stomach virus. Suki thinks she will definitely catch the virus from her friend since she saw her today.	

Skills Bank
Body Scanning   Detective Thinking
Present-moment Awareness   Problem Solving
Fun Activities   Identifying Thinking Traps

Worksheet 9.2: Science Experiment Game

Nina here! Do you remember when we talked about science experiments and practiced seeing what happened when we did a science experiment where we acted opposite (of what our emotions wanted us to do)? Today, we will walk through the steps of a science experiment again!

Fill in the steps below along with your therapist as you practice this new type of science experiment.

The science experiment we are doing is:

1. Start with a question

_____

_____

2. Make a guess

_____

_____

3. Try out my experiment

_____

_____

4. Watch how it goes

_____

_____

5. Try my experiment again!

_____

_____

Your therapist will work with you to go over these next two pages together. These pictures help us Emotion Detectives understand why it is important to experience our feelings, even with strong emotions.

We will use the example of Jack being afraid of dogs to explain how using our science experiment steps can help us face tough situations - like being around for a dog for Jack - and help ourselves feel better over time!

Emotion Curve: Avoidance/Escape

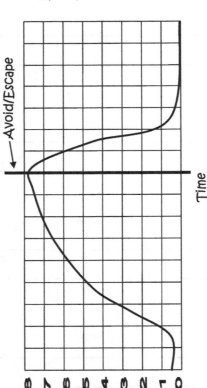

Look at this picture on the left. This might happen if Jack sees a dog, is very afraid of dogs, and runs away when he feels very scared. This running away makes his level of fear on the Emotion Thermometer go down fast, which feels good in the here and now. But, we learned earlier in this program that running away when we are scared may get us further stuck in the cycle of avoidance and make us feel more scared in the long run.

Emotion Curve: Getting used to it

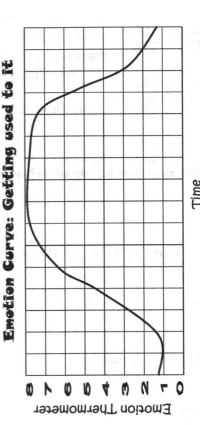

Now look at this picture on the right. If Jack doesn't avoid the dog in our example, his fear level goes down slowly over time. By letting his emotion just be there (or maybe even using his noticing, describing and experiencing it steps to help!) and not avoiding the dog, Jack's fear will go down on its own. There is a fancy word for this: **habituation!**

Figure 9.1

Another Kind of Science Experiment

Now comes the part where we learn why it is important to experience our emotions over and over again. In the first picture, you saw that Jack's fear level goes down really fast when he runs away from the dog. Since he felt better right away, it might seem like a great idea for him to keep running away from dogs. I mean, who wants to wait to feel better really slowly when you can feel better faster?

But the problem with the first picture is if Jack has to be around dogs later, he probably hasn't learned much about how to deal with them or his feelings about them. So, he will be more likely to keep running off if he sees a dog.

Let's see what can happen if Jack practices staying around dogs over and over. Look at the next picture:

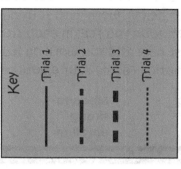

Emotion Curve: Getting Used to It with Practice

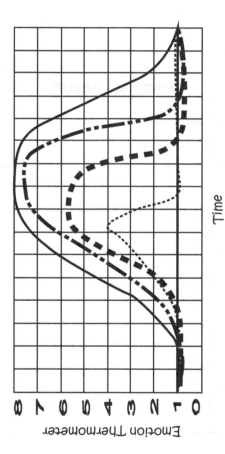

This one shows that the more Jack practices staying near dogs (safe ones, of course!), even if it is hard to do so, the more his emotion goes down and the less time it sticks around for. The more he tries to be around dogs and stays, the less Jack will be afraid of dogs!

We think this same thing will be true if you practice experiencing your tough emotions too, like anger, sadness, worry, and fear. But we don't expect you to just take our word for it. Let's start by doing some more science experiments to see if our emotions get less strong over time when we practice facing them!

Figure 9.1
Continued

Form 9.1: Emotional Behavior Form—Child Version

Work with your parent and therapist to decide when you feel strong emotions and the behaviors that your emotions make you want to do at these times. Think of things you do when you feel strong emotions, like avoid, escape, or do things that get you in trouble. Then write them next to the situation in which you experience these strong emotions. Using the Emotion Thermometer below, work with your parents, using their form to help you, to rate how much strong *emotion* you feel in each situation you come up with. You and your parents will use the last part (did you work on it?) later to write down which of these situations you tried to practice facing your emotions with!

No strong emotion	A little strong emotion	Medium strong emotion	A lot of strong emotion	Very, very strong emotion

0   1   2   3   4   5   6   7   8

Situation	Emotional Behavior	How strong is the emotion (0–8)?	Did you work on it (Y/N)?

During this session we will:

1. Learn more about using science experiments to face emotions.

2. Learn about what "safety behaviors" are

3. Practice a science experiment to face strong emotions.

4. Make plans for more science experiments to face strong emotions at home and in session.

We have learned about a few different types of science experiments that Emotion Detectives use to deal with strong emotions. Before we practice more science experiments for facing strong emotions, let's review the ones that we have learned about so far!

Facing Our Body Clues

Making ourselves feel body clues on purpose by doing things like running around or holding our breath and watching those feelings as they change over time.

Opposite Action

Doing the opposite of what our emotion wants us to do, like doing something fun when we feel sad!

Facing Our Strong Emotions

When we approach and stick with a situation that makes us feel strong emotions and makes us want to use unhelpful behaviors. For example, if we are afraid of dogs, we might try to be brave and slowly work on being around dogs anyway.

Figure 10.1

Types of Science Experiments

Sometimes we might feel like we can only face our emotions if we have a special thing or person around. As Emotion Detectives, we may want to practice facing our emotions *without* safety behaviors, because that's how we learn that we can be brave and face our emotions on our own.

Read more about safety behaviors below, and if this is one of your safety behaviors, check the box next to the description. You can talk about these more with your therapist!

Bringing Parents

All Emotion Detectives love our parents! And being around mom or dad can make anyone feel safer. However, when you are being brave and doing things that make you feel strong emotions, we want you to try to do it even without your parents being there (as long as it is safe for you to do it alone). So, if you practice facing strong emotions with mom or dad, ask them if you can try it by yourself next time or at a place like school, where your parent isn't normally there.

Do I do this?

Bringing Friends

Some Emotion Detectives use a friend to help them be brave. Having friends is great, and we want all Emotion Detectives to have friends. But, when being brave and facing tough emotions, we want you to try to also do it yourself! So, if you practice facing strong emotions with a friend, that's great! Just try it on your own too.

Do I do this?

Distraction & Bringing Things

Some Emotion Detectives try to distract themselves by thinking about or doing other things when they are faced with strong emotions (like thinking about a favorite toy or bringing a water bottle). Remember to use your Notice it, Say something about it, Experience it steps to notice that you are doing this and stay in the present moment.

Do I do this?

Figure 10.2

Safety Behaviors

Now that we Emotion Detectives have taught you all the steps of a science experiment and you have practiced lots of science experiments with your therapist and at home, we are ready to do our first **facing our emotions experiment** together in group!

Your therapist will tell you more about what experiment you will do. Just remember to write down the steps of your experiment as you go along and to use your Notice it, Say something about it, and Experience it skills, as needed, during the experiment to stay in the present moment.

1. Start by naming the activity

_____

_____

2. Make a guess

_____

_____

3. Try out my experiment

_____

_____

4. Watch how it goes

_____

_____

5. Try my experiment again!

_____

_____

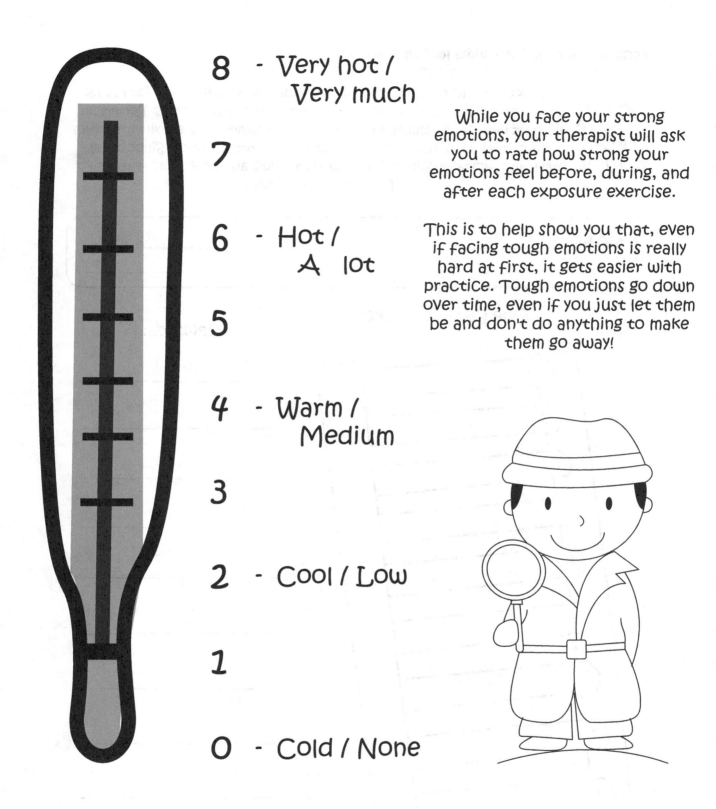

8 - Very hot /
Very much

7

While you face your strong emotions, your therapist will ask you to rate how strong your emotions feel before, during, and after each exposure exercise.

6 - Hot /
A lot

5

This is to help show you that, even if facing tough emotions is really hard at first, it gets easier with practice. Tough emotions go down over time, even if you just let them be and don't do anything to make them go away!

4 - Warm /
Medium

3

2 - Cool / Low

1

0 - Cold / None

Figure 10.3

The Emotion Thermometer

Form 10.1: My Emotion Ladder for Home Learning

 Work with your parent and therapist to decide your first goal for facing strong emotions. Then, break down that goal into smaller steps. Remember, we start with facing things that are a little bit easier before trying the really hard stuff since facing emotions gets easier with practice! Since being brave and facing emotions is hard work, you will also be getting rewards for facing tough emotions.

GOAL: _____

_____

One Step at a Time:

Rewards:

10.

9.

8.

7.

6.

5.

4.

3.

2.

1.

_____

_____

_____

_____

_____

_____

_____

_____

_____

_____

During these sessions we will:

1. Use situational emotion exposures during session to face strong emotions.

2. Work with our parents to keep practicing situational emotion exposures at home.

Hi Emotion Detective! Jack here again. Welcome back. You have done such an excellent job learning all of your Emotion Detective skills so far!

Remember that becoming an expert Emotion Detective like Nina and me takes practice! The more we practice doing things that make us feel strong emotions in these next few sessions, the less scary, sad, or uncomfortable tough situations should get!

Before we continue practicing being brave and facing strong emotions today, let's review my steps to facing strong emotions one more time!

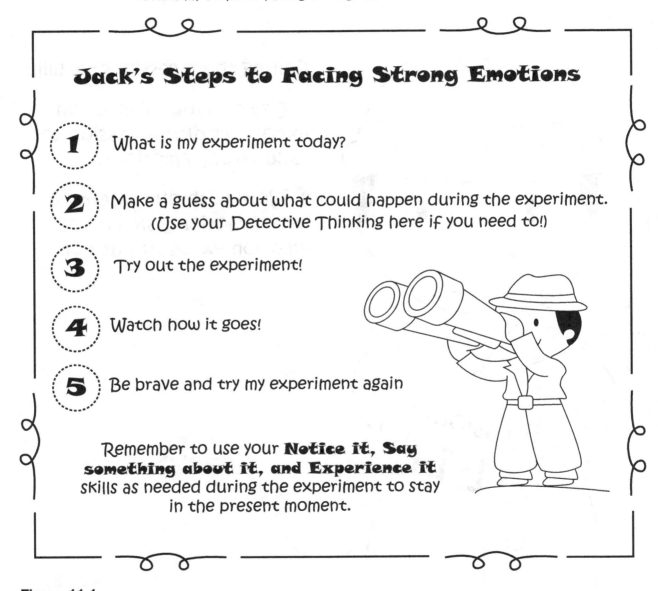

Jack's Steps to Facing Strong Emotions

1 What is my experiment today?

2 Make a guess about what could happen during the experiment. (Use your Detective Thinking here if you need to!)

3 Try out the experiment!

4 Watch how it goes!

5 Be brave and try my experiment again

Remember to use your **Notice it, Say something about it, and Experience it** skills as needed during the experiment to stay in the present moment.

Figure 11.1

Facing Strong Emotions Together—Review

Form 11.1: My Emotion Ladder for Session 11

Here's a new Emotion Ladder to use for facing strong emotions during Session 11 or for home learning after Session 11. Keep up the great work of being brave and climbing up your emotion ladders!

GOAL: _____
_____

One Step at a Time:

Rewards:

10.

9.

8.

7.

6.

5.

4.

3.

2.

1.

_____

_____

_____

_____

_____

_____

_____

_____

_____

_____

Form 11.2: My Emotion Ladder for Session 12

Just keep climbing those Emotion Ladders! Let's see if there is anything else on your Emotional Behavior Form that you can make a goal for this brand-new Emotion Ladder.

GOAL: _____
_____

One Step at a Time:

Rewards:

10.

9.

8.

7.

6.

5.

4.

3.

2.

1.

Form 11.3: My Emotion Ladder for Session 13

Time for another Emotion Ladder. Remember to look back at your Emotional Behavior Form with your therapist to figure out what another good goal might be for facing your strong emotions!

GOAL: _____
_____

One Step at a Time:

Rewards:

10.

9.

8.

7.

6.

5.

4.

3.

2.

1.

Form 11.4: My Emotion Ladder for Session 14

Wow! You have really been doing an awesome job being brave and facing strong emotions. Let's try to come up with one more goal using your Emotional Behavior Form. Great job, Emotion Detective! You've got this!

GOAL: _____
_____

One Step at a Time:

Rewards:

10.

9.

8.

7.

6.

5.

4.

3.

2.

1.

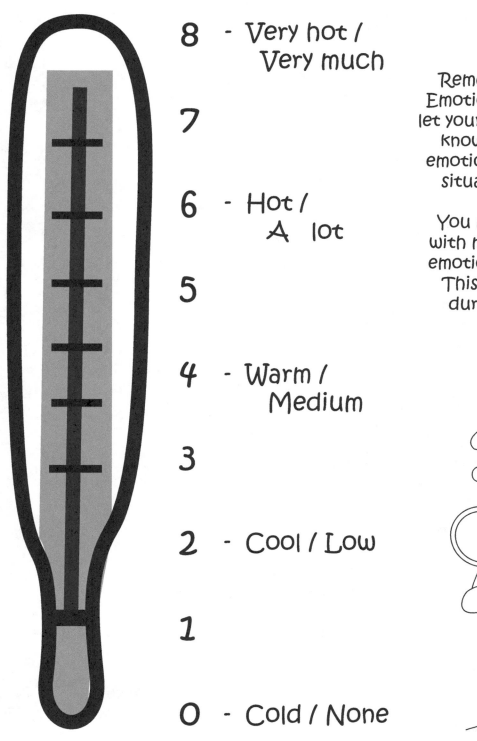

8 - Very hot /
Very much

7

6 - Hot /
A lot

5

4 - Warm /
Medium

3

2 - Cool / Low

1

0 - Cold / None

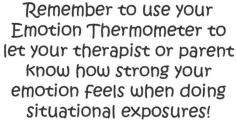

Remember to use your
Emotion Thermometer to
let your therapist or parent
know how strong your
emotion feels when doing
situational exposures!

You might notice that,
with more practice, your
emotion level goes down.
This can happen even
during the toughest
exposures!

Figure 11.2

The Emotion Thermometer

During this session we will:

1. Review skills learned in the Emotion Detectives program.

2. Plan for facing strong emotions in the future.

3. Celebrate becoming Emotion Detectives!

Session 15

You have learned so many great skills for dealing with tough emotions!

Let's spend a few minutes reviewing all the skills we have learned and the fun activities that we did to help us remember them!

My Emotion Detective Tool Kit

Skill	Fun Activities
C Skill: Consider How I Feel Emotions have three parts: feelings, thoughts, and behaviors!	True and False Alarm
	The Emotion Thermometer
	Acting Opposite Experiments
	Emotion and Activity Diary
	Finding Body Clues
	How to Body Scan
L Skill: Look at My Thoughts Remember your thinking traps!	Thinking Trap Characters
	Flexible Thinking
U Skill: Use Detective Thinking and Problem Solving Use Detective Thinking to solve thinking traps!	Mystery Game
	Detective Thinking
	Problem Solving
E Skill: Experience My Emotions How to face your strong emotions!	Notice it, Say something about it, Experience it
	Present-moment and Nonjudgmental Awareness
	Facing Strong Emotions

Figure 12.1

My Emotion Detective Tool Kit

Worksheet 12.1: Taking Stock of All I've Accomplished

You have been so brave and strong for many weeks learning to be an expert Emotion Detective! Work with your therapist to talk or write about things you did during this program, especially what made you most proud of yourself. Then, try to think about and write down things you have learned and might tell other kids about how to deal with tough emotions like feeling worried, scared, angry, or sad.

1. What will you remember most about this program?

_____

_____

_____

2. What should you do when you have a tough emotion to deal with?

_____

_____

_____

3. What would you tell other people your age who have a lot of tough or strong emotions?

_____

_____

_____

4. What do you hope for the future?

_____

_____

_____

YOU DID IT!

Worksheet 12.2: Becoming My Own Therapist!

Now that you have learned all of our Emotion Detective skills, you are ready to be your very own therapist!

You will probably still have some strong emotions sometimes (everybody does!) and, as Emotion Detectives, you should try to use your skills when you have tough emotions! Work with your therapist to make some plans for how you might continue to practice dealing with strong emotions.

1. What things or situations do you still want to work on?

_____

_____

_____

_____

_____

2. How can you deal with these things or situations?

_____

_____

_____

_____

_____

3. What skills will you use over the next few weeks to keep your progress going and keep working toward your goals?

_____

_____

_____

_____

_____

DIPLOMA

This Certificate of Excellence is presented to

_____

for outstanding completion of the UP-C Emotion Detectives Program

_____   _____
Therapist   Date

CHAPTER 13 | Consider How I Feel for Parents

(Sessions 1–4 for Parents)

SESSION 1 GOALS

- To become familiar with the structure of this treatment and the CLUES skills
- To learn about the three-component model of emotions
- To learn about the cycle of avoidance and other emotional behaviors

Getting Acquainted with Treatment

Welcome to the *Unified Protocol for Transdiagnostic Treatment of Emotional Disorders in Children* (UP-C) treatment program! This program is for children who experience strong emotions—such as sadness, anxiety, and anger—and have difficulty managing their emotions in helpful or effective ways. For many children, their emotions often feel like a mystery. Not only are emotions difficult for children to identify at times, but they often seem to come out of nowhere and may influence behavior in confusing or unwanted ways. In this treatment, your child will be learning to solve the mystery of his or her emotions by becoming what we call an "Emotion Detective." As the parent or caregiver of a child who experiences strong emotions, you too have an important role to play in this treatment. You and your child's therapist will become your child's *detective team*.

To do this, you will first need to learn the skills that your child is also learning in this treatment so that you can coach your child on when and how to use them. Your child will be learning a lot during each session, so it is important that you as a parent attend each session with your child to ensure that you understand the skills as well. This will allow you to effectively coach your child to use the skills at home. To help you remember the dates of each session, you will find a treatment schedule in Figure 13.1.

Detectives search for clues when they are trying to solve a mystery; likewise, children learn different CLUES skills in each section of this treatment to help them solve their own emotional mysteries. The CLUES skills, along with a brief description of the goals for each skill, are listed in Figure 13.2: *CLUES Skills for Parents*. We also find that it is often helpful for parents to practice applying the CLUES skills to their own emotional experiences. Not only will this will help you master the skill, but it will also allow you to empathize when your child is struggling to use a skill, because you will see what it might be like to apply these skills in your own life. Plus, we think that these skills are helpful for everyone—adult or child—because everyone struggles to manage his or her emotions sometimes!

In addition to learning the CLUES skills, your child's therapist will also introduce some helpful parenting strategies for supporting a child with strong emotions. *Parenting a child with an emotional disorder can be a frustrating and confusing process!* In this treatment, we assume that all parents are doing the best they can to help their children, but many parents can benefit from more information about how to effectively help their child deal with his or her strong emotions during difficult moments. Parents' own feelings of anxiety or frustration may unintentionally result in the use of parenting behaviors that maintain strong emotions in their child or sometimes even make their child's emotional behaviors stronger. We call these less helpful parenting behaviors *emotional parenting behaviors.* This treatment will help you to replace some of these emotional parenting behaviors with *opposite parenting behaviors* that have been shown by research to be helpful and effective. You will learn more about all of these types of parenting behaviors in the next session of this treatment.

Session 1	Session 2	Session 3	Session 4	Session 5
Session 6	Session 7	Session 8	Session 9	Session 10
Session 11	Session 12	Session 13	Session 14	Session 15

Figure 13.1

Treatment Schedule

C onsider how I feel

Major Topics: - Learning about the purpose of an emotion
- Three parts of an emotion
- Cycle of avoidance and emotional behaviors
- Acting opposite of what emotions are telling you to do

L ook at my thoughts

Major Topics: - Becoming more aware of thoughts
- Practicing flexibility in thinking

U se Detective Thinking & Problem Solving

Major Topics: - Challenging unhelpful or unrealistic thoughts
- Problem Solving

E xperience my emotions

Major Topics: - Present-moment awareness
- Situational emotion exposures

S tay happy & healthy

Major Topics: - Relapse prevention
- Celebrating accomplishments

Figure 13.2

CLUES Skills for Parents

Strong emotions can feel confusing and mysterious to both the child who experiences them and the parent. Your child's strong emotions may appear to come on suddenly, for no obvious reason, and get more intense or strong quickly. At times, you may not be sure what your child is feeling, and your child may have difficulty putting his or her experience into words. During the next session, your child will begin to practice solving the mystery of his or her emotional experiences by breaking these experiences down into their different parts.

Your child and you will learn that emotions have three different parts. The *thoughts* part of an emotion refers to what your child is saying to himself or herself that leads to feeling anxious, sad, angry, or some other emotion. For example, a child who is having trouble with friends and thinks "nobody likes me" might feel sad or down, while a child who gets into trouble at school and thinks "my teacher is so unfair to me" might feel angry. The *feelings* part of the emotion refers to clues in your child's body that tell him or her that he or she is having a strong emotion. Examples of *body clues* like this might be a racing heart and feeling shaky for anxiety; feeling tired and weak for depression; and feeling warm and tense for anger. The *behavior* part of an emotion refers to what the emotion makes your child do or want to do. For example, children who feel sad or depressed often want to be alone or sleep, while children who feel fearful or anxious may want to avoid whatever is causing the strong feeling. Finally, all emotions have a *trigger*, or something that causes them to occur or sets them into motion. Most people think of a trigger as a significant event, but triggers can also be seemingly minor events, thinking about something upsetting, hearing others talk about something upsetting, or noticing an unusual body sensation.

Use *C for Parents* (Worksheet 13.1, at the end of this session) to help identify the trigger(s) and the three parts for one of your child's recent emotional experiences. You may also find it helpful to use this form to break down some of your own emotional experiences into their three parts. Practicing on yourself can help you apply this skill to your child's experiences!

If you are anything like other parents who participate in this treatment, one reason why you decided to seek help for your child probably has to do with the way that he or she behaves when experiencing a strong emotion. In this treatment, we refer to *what* an emotion makes us want to do as an *emotional behavior*. Although your child's emotional behaviors may be causing a lot of distress or difficulty right now, emotional behaviors are not necessarily a bad thing. In fact, many emotional behaviors are quite helpful in the sense that they can protect us from dangerous situations or allow us to get our needs met. For example, running away would be a helpful emotional behavior if a speeding car were coming toward us because it would allow us to escape from danger, and crying would be a helpful emotional behavior if a loved one passed away because it would alert others to how we were feeling and allow them to help support us. However, emotional behaviors can also get us stuck in unhelpful patterns when our emotions don't fit the facts of the situation and are telling us to do more than we need to do or do things more intensely than the situation requires.

To see how emotional behaviors may get your child stuck in unhelpful cycles, let's take the example of *avoidance*—an emotional behavior commonly used by children (or adults!) who are feeling strong emotions. Your child might be feeling nervous about attending a birthday party, for example, due to not knowing who will be there. At the last minute, you agree to let your child stay home from the birthday party because he or she seems to be feeling very upset. Your child likely feels better due to not having to face the situation that is causing anxiety, and you can go about your day. However, your child's avoidance of the birthday party is likely to result in more problems in the long term. Why is this the case? First, your child is going to have to figure out how to explain to friends why he or she didn't attend the birthday party, and this will likely cause more anxiety when your child returns to school. Your child also didn't get a chance to test out any worry thoughts he or she might have had about the party, to see that the party might have been fun, or to practice talking to unfamiliar kids there. Without these opportunities it may be harder for your child to attend the next birthday party, especially since your child has just learned that avoidance actually reduced fear the first time. Plus, your child may stop getting invited to birthday parties in the future if he or she continues to skip them, resulting in more problems!

Avoidance is not the only emotional behavior that can result in problematic patterns or cycles for children. Some children may not outright avoid a situation but might rely on *safety behaviors* to reduce their anxiety or feelings of sadness, such as only attending birthday parties if a parent is present or not making eye contact when meeting new people. The problem with safety behaviors is that children often come to depend on them to get through difficult situations and don't fully learn to deal with the stress of the situation appropriately. Some children who struggle with other strong emotions such as anger or frustration may not avoid situations but instead may use verbal or physical aggression because they have difficulty sitting with uncomfortable emotions. Over the next week, begin thinking about the emotional behaviors that cause the most problems for your child and, importantly, think about the goals you are setting together with your child and his or her therapist to deal with uncomfortable emotions more helpfully.

Consider Your Child's Thoughts Feelings, and Behaviors

What happened? (Trigger)

_____

_____

_____

1. What was your child thinking about? (Thoughts)

_____

_____

_____

_____

_____

Thoughts

2. What did your child feel in his or her body? (Body Clues)

_____

_____

_____

_____

_____

Body Clues

3. What did your child do (or want to do)? (Behaviors)

_____

_____

_____

_____

_____

Behaviors

- To learn how to use Worksheet 13.2: *Double Before, During, and After* to connect your child's emotional experiences and your reactions
- To learn about four emotional parenting behaviors common to parents of children with an emotional disorder
- To learn how to decrease criticism
- To learn how to use positive reinforcement

Identifying the Double Before, During, and After

Over the past week, you have begun to practice identifying the thoughts, feelings, and behaviors that make up your child's emotional experiences. When parents first begin practicing this skill, they often find certain aspects of their child's emotions mystifying! Sometimes your child's emotions may seem to come out of nowhere, with no identifiable trigger, and escalate quickly. Sometimes you may be able to identify a trigger, but that trigger seems vastly out of proportion to your child's emotional reaction. You may also have noticed that your child has very strong urges to avoid, withdraw from, or attack whatever is causing the emotion. Parents often feel helpless when their child is experiencing a strong emotion and may struggle to know whether it is best to soothe their child, reassure their child, or give their child space to manage the emotion on his or her own. In addition, parents may naturally feel frustrated or overwhelmed themselves in these situations. When this happens, parents not only have to figure out how to respond to their child's emotions but also how to manage their own emotions in the process!

As a parent you are one of the most important people in your child's life, and how you respond to your child's emotions may impact their intensity, duration, and frequency. Just like your child will spend time in the next several sessions learning to become more aware of his or her emotions, you will also be spending time becoming aware of and monitoring your responses to your child's strong emotions. This will help you determine whether you are engaging in any emotional parenting behaviors (discussed in the next section) that you may want to consider changing.

You will be using Worksheet 13.2: *Double Before, During, and After* to begin monitoring both your child's emotional experiences and your reactions and behaviors in response to those experiences. On the top half of this worksheet, you will be indicating the details of your child's emotional experience, including the *before* (trigger), *during* (three parts of the emotion), and *after* (short- and long-term consequences of your child's behavioral response to the emotion). Short-term consequences are those that occur right away, while long-term consequences can occur days, weeks, or even months later. You will use the bottom half of this worksheet to indicate *your own emotional response* to your child's strong emotion, including your own behaviors. For this part of the worksheet, the *before* is whatever you notice about your child's emotional experience. The *during* refers to the three parts of your own emotional experience, while the *after* refers to the short- and long-term consequences you experience as a parent. Take a look at the *Sample Double Before, During, and After* (Figure 13.3) to see a completed example of this worksheet.

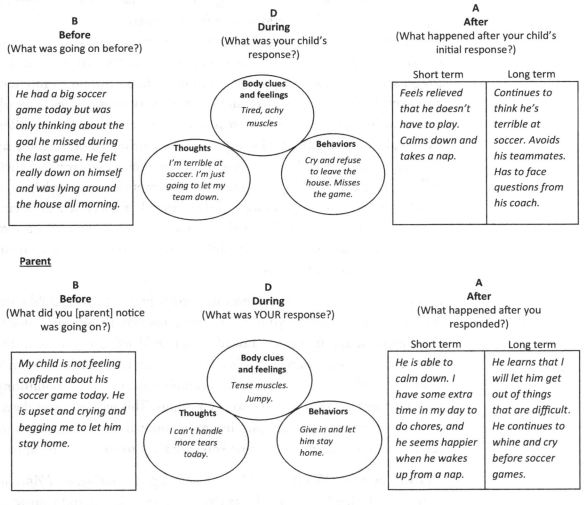

Figure 13.3

Sample Double Before, During, and After

Now, using the emotional experience you wrote about in Figure 13.2: *CLUES Skills for Parents* (or another one of your child's recent emotional experiences), complete Worksheet 13.2. Many parents notice that they respond to their child in ways that reduce their child's and their own distress in the short term but result in more distress and impairment in the long term. Do you notice this pattern happening for you and your child?

Four Emotional Parenting Behaviors

When your child experiences a strong emotion, your natural instinct as a parent is probably to do something to reduce your child's distress as quickly as possible. It is quite likely that when you completed the *Double Before, During, and After* worksheet, the parenting behaviors you listed were done with this purpose in mind. However, you may have found that the parenting strategies that seem to work for your child's siblings or that work for children who do not experience strong emotions don't seem to work as often for your child. Parenting a child who has difficulty with strong emotions can be confusing and frustrating because the strategies you use in an attempt to reduce his or her distress may seem to backfire. When this happens, you may find yourself giving in to your child when you don't want to do so, acting on your own strong emotions, or losing your temper with your child. You may also feel discouraged because it seems as though you've tried everything and nothing has worked!

In this treatment, you will be learning about four *emotional parenting behaviors* that parents tend to use during times when they are frustrated or overwhelmed by their child's emotions. Most parents use these behaviors because they are trying to help their child or reduce their child's distress. Some of these emotional parenting behaviors may actually seem to work in the short term, but in the long term they can have a negative impact on their child's emotions, behavior, and functioning. Over the course of this treatment, you will be learning to decrease your use of these emotional parenting behaviors and increase your use of what we call *opposite parenting behaviors*, which are parenting strategies shown by research to be effective in managing emotional disorders. We have including a description of each emotional parenting behavior and its opposite parenting behavior discussed in this treatment in Table 13.1: *Common Emotional Parenting Behaviors and Their Opposite Parenting Behaviors.*

Table 13.1 Common Emotional Parenting Behaviors and Their Opposite Parenting Behaviors

Emotional Parenting Behavior	Examples of Emotional Parenting Behavior	Possible Long-Term Consequences of Emotional Parenting Behavior	Opposite Parenting Behavior
Overcontrol/ Overprotection	■ Speaking for your child in social situations ■ Not allowing your child to engage in age-appropriate activities for fear something bad might happen ■ Making excuses to others for your child's withdrawal or avoidance behavior	■ Low self-esteem or self-efficacy ■ Increased avoidance ■ Poor social skills	*Healthy Independence-Granting*
Criticism	■ Paying a lot of attention to your child's mistakes or misbehaviors ■ Focusing on the negative aspects of your child's behavior and ignoring the positive aspects ■ Subtle behaviors such as eye rolling, head shaking, or sighing ■ Telling your child that he or she shouldn't feel a certain way or should stop feeling a certain way	■ Low self-esteem or self-efficacy ■ Down mood ■ Gives up easily ■ Tries overly hard to please people ■ Behavior problems	*Combining Positive Reinforcement with Active Ignoring* *Expressing Empathy*
Inconsistency	■ Not following through with rewards when promised ■ Punishing naughty behavior sometimes but allowing your child to get away with it at other times ■ Frequently changing household rules ■ Encouraging *approach behaviors* at certain times and *avoidance behaviors* at other times	■ More behavior problems ■ Less compliance with your rules and expectations ■ More avoidance or other emotional behaviors ■ Increased anxiety	*Using Consistent Discipline and Praise*
Excessive Modeling of Strong Emotions and Avoidance	■ Extreme reactions to and avoidance of situations that are not really threatening ■ Expressing adult worries in front of your child ■ Hiding your emotions or refusing to talk about sad events that impact the family ■ Using aggressive behaviors or swearing excessively when angry ■ Isolating yourself from your family when angry or upset	■ More frequent negative emotions, such as anxiety, sadness, or anger ■ More intense expression of negative emotions *Or* ■ Difficulty expressing emotions ■ Avoids discussing negative emotions	*Healthy Emotional Modeling*

Think of a time when your boss, coworker, or family member criticized you in some way. Do you recall how you felt? What about how that criticism impacted your behavior—do you recall that? Now, think of a time when you were praised for something you did. How did you feel and act? Which was more motivating—the criticism or the praise? Which resulted in a more significant and long-lasting change in your behavior?

For most of us, criticism brings up a host of negative emotions. It may result in feeling sad and discouraged, leading us to give up or not try as hard the next time. Or it may result in anger and defensiveness, both of which stop us from taking a look at what happened to see what we could do differently the next time. Critical behaviors or comments have the same impact upon your child's emotions and behaviors. In fact, they may have even more of an impact, as research shows that children who struggle with strong emotions are more sensitive to criticism and are more likely to perceive neutral comments or behaviors as critical. Most parents do not set out to be critical of their children. In fact, parents of children with emotional disorders may be more careful than other parents about not criticizing their child, as they do not want to say or do anything to increase their child's distress. Nevertheless, many parents (and teachers and coaches and friends) are unaware of the very subtle behaviors or statements that may be perceived as criticism by their emotional child.

Take a look at the following types of statements and behaviors that might be perceived as criticism by your child. Think about whether you use any of these types of statements or behaviors in an effort to manage your child's strong emotions. Some of these types of criticism may seem quite obvious to you, but others may be surprising.

- *Global Negative Statements*: "You're always so shy!" *Or* "Why can't you ever do anything for yourself?"
- *Negative Statements about a Specific Behavior*: "You didn't do very well on this assignment, did you?" *Or* "You looked like you were sleeping on that field today!"
- *Focusing on the Negative Aspects of a Behavior and Ignoring the Positive*: "I can't believe you're having a tantrum right now after such a good week! *Or* "I know you can do better than a B+ next time."
- *Dismissing Your Child's Feelings*: "Cheer up! There's nothing to be sad about." *Or* "I just can't understand why you're so angry about this!"
- *Subtle Critical Behaviors*: Eye rolling, shaking your head, sighing loudly

All parents make critical statements sometimes, so if any of these sound familiar to you then you are not alone. In the next section, you will learn about the opposite parenting behavior of pairing active ignoring with positive reinforcement.

Increasing Positive Reinforcement

Many parents of children with strong emotions, whether or not they use much criticism, pay a lot of attention to the things that are going wrong. This is natural—after all, you are here because there are some things that are not going very well for your child right now! However, paying a lot of attention during times when your child is misbehaving or struggling with strong emotions can sometimes make things worse. This is because your child desires your attention more than almost anything else. Therefore, he or she will continue to do the things that get your attention, even if the type of attention your child is getting is negative or even critical. Conversely, your attention is a powerful tool that you can use to your advantage! By paying a lot of attention to the times when your child is trying to use skills, expressing emotions appropriately, or behaving well, you can increase the chances that your child will continue to do these things in the future. At the same time, by choosing not to attend to your child when he or she is expressing emotions inappropriately or misbehaving in minor ways, you decrease the likelihood that your child will continue to do these things in the future.

There are many effective ways of attending to your child when your child is doing something you want him or her to keep doing. These vary from simple changes in your behavior such as facing your child or making eye contact, to statements that express praise and approval, to actually rewarding your child for positive behaviors or effective coping. You will be learning a bit more about all of these strategies for reinforcing your child in the next session. For now, you and your child will be making a rewards list together. The purpose of this list is to come up with a variety of small rewards that your child can earn throughout treatment for trying difficult things, facing his or her fears, or practicing skills in emotional situations. These rewards should not be expensive. Although you and your child may choose to put things like small toys or treats on this list, the most valuable rewards are often things like doing activities with the family or playing a game with a parent. Some parents are concerned that once they start rewarding their child for something, they will have to keep doing it indefinitely. *This is not the case.* Once your child is successful in a situation, you can begin to phase out the use of rewards.

Worksheet 13.2: Double Before, During, and After

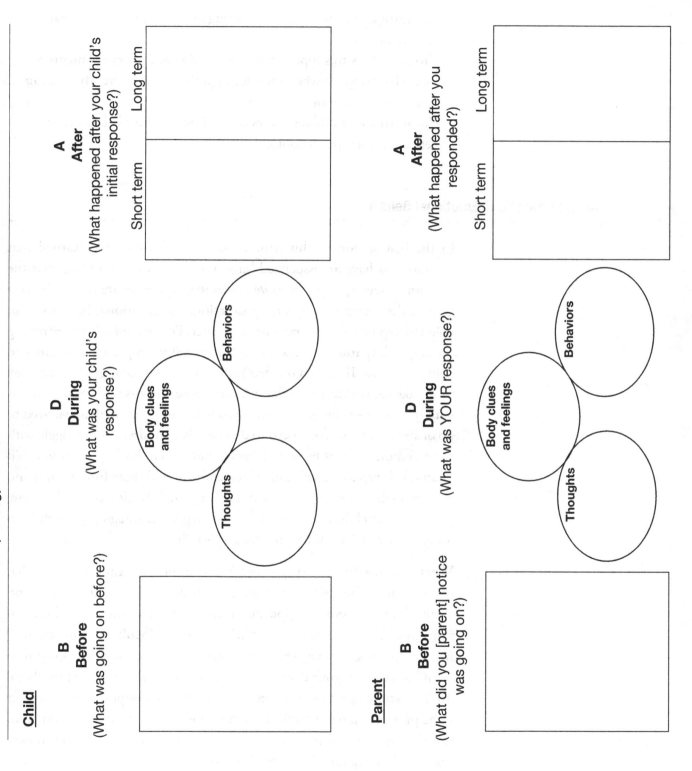

Child

B
Before
(What was going on before?)

D
During
(What was your child's response?)

Body clues and feelings

Thoughts

Behaviors

A
After
(What happened after your child's initial response?)

Short term | Long term

Parent

B
Before
(What did you [parent] notice was going on?)

D
During
(What was YOUR response?)

Body clues and feelings

Thoughts

Behaviors

A
After
(What happened after you responded?)

Short term | Long term

- To learn about the concept of acting opposite to an emotional behavior
- To learn how to support children in using science experiments to see what happens when they act opposite to or differently from an emotional behavior
- To learn about different ways to reinforce positive behaviors or effective attempts at coping

Acting Opposite to Emotional Behaviors

In the first session of this treatment, you and your child learned that all emotions have an associated "emotional behavior," meaning that the emotion is trying to get us to *do something*. When we are in a truly dangerous, threatening, or upsetting situation, our emotional behaviors can help to keep us safe or to get our needs met. For example, if an oncoming car is speeding toward us, we need fear to tell us to get away in order to help protect us. If a loved one has passed away, our feelings of sadness tell us to take some time off so that we can grieve our loss and come to terms with it. However, sometimes emotions tell us to do more than we need to do or something we don't need to do at all. For children who struggle with strong emotions, this tends to happen quite often, leading them to avoid or attack things that aren't truly threatening or withdraw from friends and activities when nothing truly sad has happened. In situations like these, you and your child's detective team will begin encouraging your child to *act opposite* to what his or her emotion is telling him or her to do.

What does it mean to *act opposite*? Acting opposite means noticing what our emotional behaviors are telling us to do and, instead of acting on them, doing something opposite or very different from what the emotion says. Acting opposite will likely be very difficult for your child at first because urges to engage in emotional behaviors are often difficult to resist, especially if your child has gotten into the habit of acting on them. To help you begin to encourage your child to act opposite to his or her unhelpful emotional behaviors, we have included a list of common emotional behaviors and their opposite actions in Table 13.2. As you review this list, think about which emotional behaviors your child struggles with the most, as well as how you can begin to encourage your child to do something opposite or different when the emotion arises.

Table 13.2 Common Emotional Behaviors and Their Opposite Actions

Emotion	Emotional Behaviors	Opposite Actions
Fear	Escape	Approaching the situation or thing
Anxiety	Avoidance	Approaching the situation or thing
	Distraction	Attending to the situation or thing
	Procrastination	Starting right away
Sadness	Withdrawing from activities	Participating in activities when sad
	Avoiding people	Spending time with friends or family
	Laying around	Doing a physical activity
Anger	Attacking	Taking a "time out" for a few minutes
	Yelling and screaming	Speaking in a calm voice

Using Science Experiments to Act Opposite

Many children struggle with acting opposite, not only because it is difficult to ignore an emotional behavior but also because when stuck in a strong emotion it is hard to see at first how acting opposite to it might help. After all, your child initially feels better when he or she avoids something that provokes anxiety, and getting up and doing something active is often the last thing your child wants to do when he or she feels depressed. This week, your child will be doing a science experiment to see what happens when he or she tries out a new or different behavior when experiencing a strong emotion. Thinking about acting opposite as a science experiment will help your child keep an open mind about what might happen when trying out a new behavior. All good science experiments begin with a question. In this case, the question your child will be asking is, "How would I feel if I did something different from what I usually do when I feel sad, bored, anxious, or angry?" Your child will then come up with a hypothesis about how it might feel to act opposite to the emotional behavior, and then do an experiment to test out this hypothesis.

Because nearly everyone can relate to feeling sad, down, or bored some of the time, your child will begin by doing a science experiment that focuses on acting opposite to these types of emotions. As Table 13.2 illustrates, when children feel sad or down they often want to be by themselves, withdraw from activities, or lay around a lot. The problem with acting on these emotional behaviors is that it doesn't do anything to change the emotion (and often makes the emotion worse!), and it can lead to problems with friendships, activities, or schoolwork. We want to teach children that sometimes the best way to change their emotion is to change their activity level or change what they're doing when they experience the emotion, rather than waiting for their emotion to change.

To become more aware of the connection between emotions and activities, your child will be completing Worksheet 3.5: *My Emotion and Activity Diary*, located in the child section of this workbook. This worksheet will allow your child to track the connection between his or her emotions, the number of activities, and the types of activities he or she engages in each day. Twice this coming week, when feeling bored, sad, or down, your child will do an experiment by acting opposite to his or her emotional behavior by choosing to engage in an enjoyable or meaningful activity. In this session, your child will be coming up with a list of enjoyable activities he or she can do during these experiments or at any time when he or she is feeling sad or down (Worksheet 3.4: *My Activities List* in the child section of this workbook). These activities might come from a variety of categories, including *service activities* (doing things for others), *mastery activities* (learning new things), *social activities* (doing things with people), or *physical activities* (moving their bodies).

What can you as a parent do this week to help your child with these home learning assignments? First, you can help your child establish a time each day to complete Worksheet 3.5: *My Emotion and Activity Diary*. The most helpful time to do this is often at the end of the day, although your child may benefit from your help in recalling activities done and emotions experienced over the course of the day. Because acting opposite to strong emotions can be very difficult to do, your child will also likely need help in completing two science experiments this week. One way you can do this is by helping your child identify times when he or she typically struggles with feelings of sadness or boredom, and then helping your child identify an activity to do during this time. Another approach would be to point out when you notice your child engaging in emotional behaviors consistent with sadness or boredom, and then help him or her choose an activity to do in the moment. Whatever approach you take, it is often helpful to ask your child to make a hypothesis about what he or she thinks might happen after acting opposite to the emotional behavior, have your child rate his or her level of emotion before and after, and then ask your child to evaluate whether his or her hypothesis was correct.

Last week, you and your child began creating a rewards list at the end of session to identify small rewards your child can earn for practicing brave behaviors, implementing skills learned in treatment, or acting opposite to difficult emotions. If you have already begun to use these rewards at home with your child—then great! If not, you may want to start rewarding your child this week for doing science experiments to see what happens when he or she acts opposite to his or her emotional behaviors when feeling sad, down, or bored. As discussed already, acting opposite to strong emotions can be very difficult, and your child may require some extra reinforcement in order to do so.

There are many ways to reinforce your child in addition to the rewards that you came up with together during the last session. Take a look at *10 Ways to Reinforce Your Child* (Worksheet 13.3) for some suggestions. When they first begin using rewards, many parents feel frustrated with having to reward their child for activities they feel their child should already be doing successfully on his or her own, without extra encouragement. It may seem odd to reward your child for doing something fun when feeling sad, let alone for things like taking a shower, starting homework, or attending a social event. It is important to remember that your child is not doing these things independently because they are difficult or bring up strong emotions, so you need to meet your child where he or she is at. Once your child is doing these activities successfully, you will be able to phase out the reward. Until then, it is important to consistently reinforce whatever behavior you would like to see your child do more of.

Use Worksheet 13.3: *10 Ways to Reinforce Your Child* to identify how you will reward your child this week for completing his or her opposite action science experiments. At the bottom of the worksheet, there is a space for you to write down which reward or rewards you plan to use, as well as your child's response to those rewards.

For your home learning assignment this week, you should also complete one *Double Before During, and After* worksheet (Worksheet 13.4) for an emotional experience that occurs for your child this week.

Worksheet 13.3: 10 Ways to Reinforce Your Child

(1) **Praise** your child for the successful behavior or the behavior you want to see more. The most effective type of praise is labeled praise, which tells your child not only that you liked something he or she did but also what exactly you liked.

  Example: "Thank you for joining us for family game night even though you're feeling sad."
  Or "I like how you stayed calm when your sister was getting on your nerves."

(2) Use **nonverbal cues** to communicate to your child that you like what he or she is doing. Nonverbal cues can include looking at your child, smiling, nodding, or clapping your hands.

(3) Give your child a **sticker or star** every time he or she uses the behavior or skill you want to see more. You can create a sticker or star chart for your child and, after he or she has earned a designated number of stickers or stars, reward your child with a prize.

(4) Establish a **token jar** and place a token in it every time your child uses the behavior or skill you want. When your child earns a certain number of tokens, he or she may earn a prize.

(5) Allow your child to choose a **favorite meal** for dinner or let him or her **pick a movie** or television show for the family to watch.

(6) Make time for you and your child to do a **special activity alone together**, without siblings or other family members involved. Having a parent's full, undivided attention can be very reinforcing!

(7) Give your child a small **toy or treat** of his or her choice.

(8) Allow your child to earn extra **screen time** (e.g., videogame time, computer time, iPad time) for engaging in target behaviors.

(9) Allow your child to stay up an hour past his or her bedtime on a school night (or allow your child to do something else that he or she doesn't normally get to do).

(10) Give your child a **hug or high five**.

Write down two types of reinforcements you plan to use this week when your child does his or her science experiments:

_____   _____

How did your child respond to these reinforcements?_____

_____

What other behaviors did you reinforce this week? What types of reinforcement did you use?

_____

_____

Worksheet 13.4: Double Before, During, and After

Child

B
Before
(What was going on before?)

D
During
(What was your child's response?)

Body clues and feelings

Behaviors

Thoughts

A
After
(What happened after your child's initial response?)

Short term   Long term

Parent

B
Before
(What did you [parent] notice was going on?)

D
During
(What was YOUR response?)

Body clues and feelings

Behaviors

Thoughts

A
After
(What happened after you responded?)

Short term   Long term

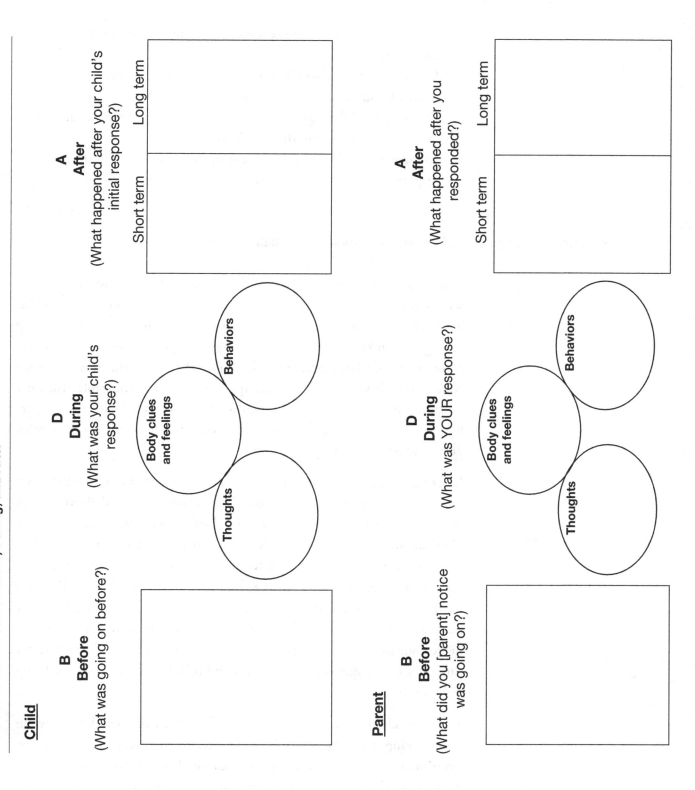

- To learn how children express and experience emotions in their bodies
- To learn how to help children scan their bodies to become more aware of body sensations
- To understand the rationale for sensational exposures and support children in completing them at home
- To learn about the opposite parenting behavior of expressing empathy when children are struggling with strong emotions

How Children Express and Experience Emotions in Their Bodies

It is Sunday evening, and your child is approaching a stressful week at school with a big test and several projects due. All weekend, your child has been avoiding schoolwork, spending time with friends and playing videogames instead. As the evening progresses, your child begins to complain of a headache and feeling sick to his or her stomach. Although your child doesn't have a fever, he or she appears to be uncomfortable. The next morning, things appear to be much the same. Is your child sick, or perhaps just anxious about the upcoming week at school? If he or she asks, do you allow your child to stay home?

Most parents, including parents of children without emotional disorders, have found themselves in a situation like the one described above. When children experience strong emotions, they sometimes express them as physical complaints. For example, a child who is anxious may complain that his tummy hurts or that he feels dizzy; a child who is sad may complain that she feels tired or achy; a child who is frustrated may talk about feeling hyper, restless, or tense. During these times, your child may or may not be able to identify the emotion he or she is feeling. This can make your role as a parent quite confusing! You may also feel frustrated at times because it may seem like your child is "faking" symptoms or being difficult on purpose.

Typically, children complain of physical feelings in their bodies when experiencing a strong emotion either because they are unaware of the emotion they are experiencing or because they do not know how to describe it. They just know that they are feeling very uncomfortable!

While some children may be overly aware of sensations in their bodies, other children may completely lack awareness of body sensations. Not only may they be unaware of how their bodies feel when they are anxious or sad or angry, they might also have difficulty noticing other body sensations like hunger, fullness, or pain. In fact, it can even be difficult for some adults to notice the body sensations they are having when they are upset! Maybe your child lacks this type of body awareness too or, on the other hand, seems quite sensitive to it. Or maybe—like many children—your child is somewhere in the middle.

In this session of treatment, your child will learn more about the body sensations he or she experiences with different emotions, which he or she may not seem completely aware of at the present time. We call these sensations "body clues" because they are clues to the emotion or emotions your child is experiencing. Your child will be completing several exercises to become better at noticing and describing body clues, as well as connecting them to emotional experiences. You will learn these exercises in this session too so that you can be your child's "detective sidekick" and help your child become more aware of what happens in his or her body during different emotions.

Learning to Body Scan

The first tool your child will be learning in this session to become more aware of his or her body clues is called **body scanning**. Body scanning is a type of present-moment awareness practice, or a practice that helps us to become more aware of what is happening right here in the here and now. You and your child will be learning more about present-moment awareness in Session 8 of this treatment, but for now it is helpful to know that when we practice this type of awareness, we are *noticing* what is happening, *saying something about it* (either to ourselves or out loud), and *experiencing* it without trying to push it away or avoid it. Body scanning is a way of noticing our body clues, saying something about them to help us understand them better, and experiencing them without trying to get rid of them. Body scanning is an important tool in this treatment because before children can decide what to do about their emotions—whether to act on them or not—they need to become aware that they are experiencing them in the first place!

Body scanning is a simple exercise that can be practiced anywhere and doesn't require any special supplies. However—this doesn't mean it is easy to do! It is easy to become distracted during body scanning, and many children find it very difficult at first to just sit and notice body clues without doing anything about them. Encourage your child to practice body scanning this week—both during times when your child seems calm and relaxed and during times when your child is experiencing a strong emotion. Directions for body scanning are provided below, but you may need to adjust these directions to make them most useful for your child.

Steps for Body Scanning

1. Close your eyes and focus your attention on your body.
2. Starting at the tip-top of your head, slowly move down your body. Notice any parts of your body that feel tight or uncomfortable. Make sure you move all the way down to your toes.
3. As you notice each body clue, rate how strong each one is on a 0-to-8 scale.
4. Say something to yourself about what each body clue feels like.
5. Experience each body clue by sticking with the feeling, even if it is uncomfortable.
6. After you have practiced experiencing your body clues, now rate again how strong each one is. What do you notice?

As your child describes each body clue, it may be helpful to ask him or her questions about what each clue feels like to encourage your child to describe his or her body clues as fully as possible. If you notice that your child is describing body clues using negative terms (e.g., "my stomach feels yucky"), encourage your child to focus on just describing the sensation (e.g., "my stomach is moving around a lot and feels like it's doing somersaults"). If you notice your child becoming distracted or trying to avoid body clues, gently bring your child's attention back to his or her body. Point out any changes your child describes in his or her body clues over the course of body scanning.

Understanding and Practicing Sensational Exposures

The body clues your child experiences when he or she is feeling a strong emotion are often uncomfortable, and it makes sense that your child would want to do something to reduce these body clues and get rid of the strong emotions as quickly as possible. Although this is a natural response to experiencing a strong emotion, it is not often the most helpful or effective thing to do. Although uncomfortable, body clues are not dangerous or harmful, and your child never has a chance to learn this if he or she immediately tries to do something to get rid of them. Your child also does not learn that he or she has the ability to tolerate the physical sensations associated with strong emotions, or that these sensations will naturally reduce on their own over time. One important goal for this session is for your child to learn that emotions are not harmful, they can be handled even when they are intense, and they do not last forever!

To learn this, your child will be participating in some exercises called *sensational exposures*. A sensational exposure is an activity done with the purpose of bringing on strong body sensations associated with different emotions so that your child can practice noticing them, sitting with them, and waiting for them to reduce naturally. Before, right after, and several minutes after participating in sensational exposures, your child will be asked to do body scanning and to rate his or her level of uncomfortable physical feelings. Some children find these activities very distressing, while others do not find them distressing at all.

At least once this week, work with your child to practice a sensational exposure, using the list in Table 13.3. You can choose one that you believe will bring on physical sensations similar to those your child experiences during strong emotions, or you can ask your child's therapist which one he or she recommends. Have your child practice body scanning and rate the intensity of his or her physical sensations (body clues) before,

Table 13.3 Ideas for Sensational Exposures at Home

Sensational Exposure Activity	Body Clues Associated with Activity
Shake head from side to side for 30 seconds	Dizziness, blurred vision
Run in place for 1 minute/50 jumping jacks	Racing heart, sweating
Hold breath for 30 seconds	Shortness of breath, chest tightness
Spin for 1 minute	Dizziness, blurred vision
Wall sit for 30 seconds	Muscle weakness, fatigue
Place head between knees for 30 seconds and then lift	Dizziness

right after, and several minutes after the exposure. For their home learning assignment, your child will use *Finding Your Body Clues at Home* (Worksheet 4.2) to indicate body clues he or she noticed during the sensational exposure.

Opposite Parenting Behavior: Expressing Empathy When Your Child is Struggling

So far, we have been focusing in this session on your child's distress when experiencing strong physical sensations and emotions. However, it is important not to overlook the fact that parents often feel frustrated, stressed, or upset when their child is experiencing frequent and strong emotions, especially if these emotions are accompanied by high levels of body distress and avoidance. Many parents believe that it is helpful to minimize or deny their child's complaints, especially if their child's emotions are interfering with daily life or making it hard to get things done. For example, you might find yourself saying things like "there's nothing to be sad about" if your child is crying over a seemingly minor incident, or "your stomach ache isn't really that bad" if your child is complaining of stomach pain on the way to school.

Parents often make these types of statements with the well-intentioned objective of reducing their child's attention to emotions and uncomfortable body clues that are getting in the way or causing problems for both the child and the parent. However, these types of statements can be subtle forms of criticism (one of our emotional parenting behaviors) and can have unintended negative consequences. Comments like these may suggest to your child that he or she shouldn't be feeling certain emotions. As we discussed in the first session of this treatment, *all* emotions are normal, natural, and not harmful, and it is therefore important to send your child the message that no emotions are bad. Your child may be having trouble expressing an emotion in an effective or appropriate way, but that doesn't mean the emotion itself is wrong or unwarranted. Comments that deny or minimize emotions can also make your child start to doubt his or her own perceptions about how he or she feels. Awareness of emotions is really important in this treatment, as children cannot learn to effectively manage their emotions if they don't have a good understanding of them in the first place.

Finally, we know from research that denying, minimizing, or suppressing emotions doesn't make them go away—often, these types of avoidance make the emotion stronger. We want your child to learn to manage emotions as they come up so that they don't become a bigger problem later.

How can you as a parent acknowledge your child's emotions in the moment and encourage your child to do something to manage those emotions effectively? One way to do this is to begin to practice a skill we call **expressing empathy** for your child's emotional experience. Many parents are already quite good at being empathetic and understanding when their children are experiencing strong emotions, but it can nevertheless be helpful to learn some steps for doing so. This is especially the case for times when your child's emotional behaviors may make it difficult to be empathetic. For example, if your child is breaking rules or constantly asking for reassurance when he or she is upset, it could be challenging to figure out how to show empathy appropriately, especially if this behavior is making you feel frustrated or angry as well. It is important to remember that expressing empathy does not mean that you believe your child is expressing emotion in an appropriate or effective way. Rather, when you express empathy you communicate that you understand how your child is feeling and why your child might be feeling that way, given the situation.

Take a look at *Empathizing with Your Child's Struggle* (Worksheet 13.5). On this worksheet, you will find a step-by-step approach for expressing empathy when your child is experiencing a strong emotion. Follow these steps at least twice this week when your child appears upset, is experiencing strong body clues, or is complaining of feeling strong emotions. Note the situation, what you said, and how your child responded.

This week, you should also continue to complete one *Double Before, During, and After* (Worksheet 13.6) for a time when your child experiences a strong emotion.

Worksheet 13.5: Empathizing with Your Child's Struggle

It can be hard to express empathy when your child is overwhelmed by strong emotions, especially if you feel that your child is overreacting or managing his or her emotions in an ineffective or inappropriate way. Use the following steps to show that you understand your child's emotional experience.

(1) *Label the emotion you perceive your child to be experiencing*
      (e.g., "It looks like you are feeling sad right now")

Note that if your child rejects your emotion label and reports a different emotion, it is important to express acceptance, even if you disagree.

(2) *Communicate that you understand why your child might feel this way, given the trigger or situation*
      (e.g., "It makes sense that getting a C on a test you studied really hard for would make you feel sad")

Note that you may be having difficulty understanding your child's emotional response or feel that it is out of proportion to the trigger. It is of course okay to feel this way, but one important part of empathy is acknowledging that your child's emotion makes sense from your child's perspective.

(3) *Encourage your child to use one of his or her skills and support your child in doing so*
When your child is experiencing a strong emotion, he or she may have difficulty thinking flexibly about which skills to use or recalling how to use skills in the moment. You can help your child by suggesting and guiding your child in using skills.

Home Learning

Situation 1	Situation 2
Trigger:	Trigger:
Emotion Your Child Experienced:	Emotion Your Child Experienced:
How You Expressed Empathy:	How You Expressed Empathy:

Worksheet 13.6: Double Before, During, and After

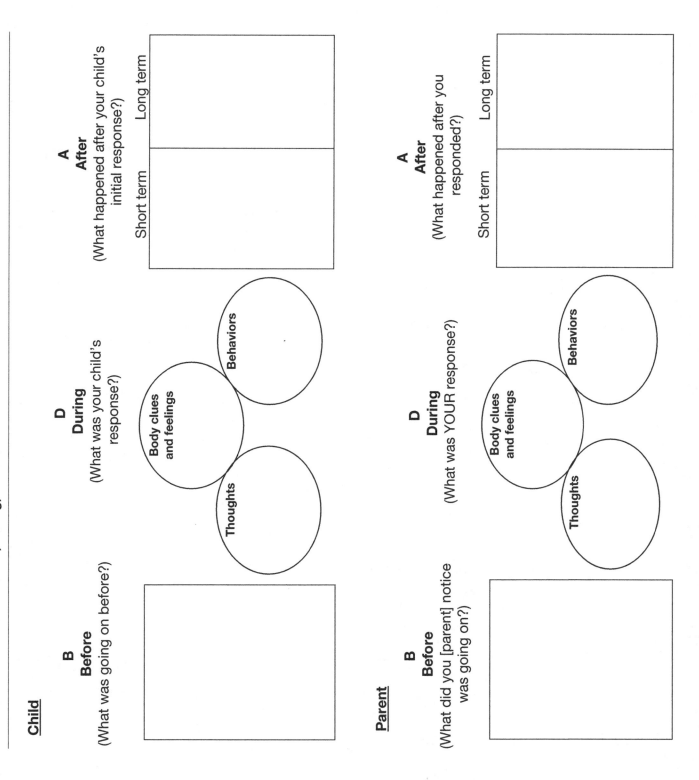

Child

B
Before
(What was going on before?)

D
During
(What was your child's response?)

Body clues and feelings

Thoughts

Behaviors

A
After
(What happened after your child's initial response?)

Short term

Long term

Parent

B
Before
(What did you [parent] notice was going on?)

D
During
(What was YOUR response?)

Body clues and feelings

Thoughts

Behaviors

A
After
(What happened after you responded?)

Short term

Long term

CHAPTER 14

Look at My Thoughts for Parents

(Session 5 for Parents)

SESSION 5 GOALS

- To learn how thinking flexibly can help your child reduce strong emotions
- To learn about four thinking traps that get children with strong emotions stuck
- To learn about different types of reinforcement and punishment
- To be able to identify the problems resulting from inconsistent discipline and praise
- To learn strategies for practicing more consistent discipline and praise in your household

Flexible Thinking and Strong Emotions

Take a moment to consider all the decisions you make in your daily life without even thinking much about them. From deciding what to wear to your route to work to your bedtime routine, you probably make hundreds of decisions each day automatically, with little to no effort. This is because you have encountered these same situations so many times that you have developed shortcuts—sometimes called *heuristics*—for navigating them effortlessly. Heuristics are often very helpful, as they free up time and mental resources to focus on more important things that do require attention and careful thought. However, our heuristics can sometimes be incorrect, leading us to interpret the world inaccurately and act on our interpretations in unhelpful ways.

In this session and the next portion of treatment, you and your child will focus on identifying and changing the inaccurate and unhelpful heuristics or thinking patterns your child uses when experiencing strong emotions. Situations that evoke strong emotions often grab our attention, to the exclusion of everything else. This makes a lot of sense: if we were in a truly threatening or upsetting situation (in other words, experiencing a true alarm), we would want to focus intensely on the emotional aspect of the situation in order to quickly assess the threat and do something about it. We would not want to spend too much time thinking about it; pondering the situation might get in the way of getting to safety or communicating our needs as quickly as possible. However, when we are in a false-alarm situation (in other words, a situation that is not truly upsetting or dangerous even though our emotion tells us it is), acting quickly on our "gut" interpretations of our emotions can cause problems.

Your child has already begun to identify the thoughts he or she experiences during strong emotions. This practice will come in handy this session, where your child will learn to evaluate whether his or her thoughts fall into any unhelpful or inaccurate thinking patterns common to children with emotional disorders. The overarching goal of this session (focusing on the L skill) and the next two (focusing on the U skill) is to teach your child that his or her **snap judgments** about emotional situations may not always be accurate and to help your child think more flexibly about these types of situations.

Common Thinking Traps

We call the shortcuts or heuristics children use to interpret false-alarm situations **thinking traps** because they are thought patterns your child tends to get stuck in when he or she encounters an emotional situation. Researchers and therapists who work with children and adults have found that certain types of thinking traps tend to be especially common in people who experience strong feelings of anxiety, sadness, or anger. Take a look at four of these common thinking traps on Worksheet 14.1: *L for Parents* (at the end of this chapter). We have provided examples of each thinking trap based on typical emotional situations that sometimes come up for adults or parents.

Over the next week, use Worksheet 14.1 to provide an example of each thinking trap for both yourself and your child. Next week, your child will begin working on changing these types of thoughts so that they are more accurate, realistic, or helpful.

Introduction to Learned Behaviors: Reinforcement and Punishment

Children who struggle with strong emotions often seem to behave in unpredictable and mysterious ways, creating understandable confusion for their parents! Maybe you have had the experience of your child sailing through a situation you thought would provoke significant anxiety, or the experience of your child becoming very upset by a situation you thought would not be a big deal. You may have also had the experience of your child misbehaving in some situations but being on his or her best behavior in others. These inconsistencies in your child's emotions and behaviors can seem quite mysterious, but the answers to these mysteries may lie in how you and others have responded to your child's emotions and behaviors in the past.

Reinforcement, which we have already begun to discuss in previous sessions, means adding or giving something pleasant or desirable after your child has behaved in a certain way, making your child more likely to show or do that behavior again. *Punishment* means using a consequence after your child has behaved in a certain way, making your child less likely to demonstrate that behavior again. Adults can and do *accidentally* reinforce naughty behaviors in children and punish desirable behaviors. However, once you understand these concepts better, you will likely feel in better control of your child's emotions and behaviors because you will be able to carefully choose what to reinforce and what to punish.

Take a look at Worksheet 14.2: *Understanding Learned Behaviors*, which lists the two different types of reinforcement and two different types of punishment. You will find some examples of reinforcement and punishment on this worksheet, and there is also space to write in your own examples. Use this worksheet for this week's home learning assignment to write down examples of ways you use each type of reinforcement and punishment during the next week. If you find that you do not use all four types, try to think of an example or two from the past.

In most situations, your most effective first-line discipline strategy will be using *positive reinforcement when your child does something you would like to see more* and *actively ignoring behaviors you would like to see less.* For example, you might praise your child whenever you notice her playing nicely with her sibling and ignore minor squabbles by not giving them any attention. You have already begun to practice this approach, which can be applied during times when your child is experiencing strong emotions too. For example, you might praise your child for going to a friend's birthday party even when he feels down but ignore your child's repeated complaints about how tired he is feeling when you know he has gotten enough sleep. Of course, sometimes your child may break a rule that cannot be ignored, such as if he or she becomes aggressive with a sibling or breaks something in thve house on purpose. During these times when you cannot ignore a misbehavior, using punishment may be necessary.

Emotional Parenting Behavior: Inconsistent Discipline/Praise

Both reinforcement and punishment work best when you use them *consistently* or routinely in response to your child's behavior so that your child has ample opportunity to learn the association between his or her behavior and the consequence. However, these strategies can sometimes backfire if you use them inconsistently. In the case of rewards, your child may lose motivation to keep doing a desirable behavior if he or she is only rewarded for it sometimes or if the rewards stop before the behavior has become routine. If you don't always follow through with punishments, your child may get the message that you're not serious about them and continue to misbehave.

Some parents also end up accidentally reinforcing behaviors they don't intend to reinforce, without realizing that they are doing so. For example, imagine that you are in the grocery store checkout aisle, and your son asks you to buy him a candy bar. When you say "no," he begins to whine. You don't respond, and as a result he whines louder and louder. Becoming embarrassed and not wanting to make a scene, you reluctantly agree to purchase the candy bar. What behavior do you think you have just reinforced? If you said whining loudly, you would be correct. Without even knowing it, you have just taught your child that to get a candy bar next time, he just needs to whine loudly enough. As this example illustrates, when you are reinforcing your child, it is important to think about what behaviors you are reinforcing. And remember that reinforcements can include not only tangible desired items but also your attention and verbal responses.

Many of the parents who participate in this treatment lead quite busy and hectic lives, which often makes it difficult to maintain consistency with rewards and punishments. When you are exhausted in the evening from work, childcare, or other obligations, you may easily forget to add a sticker to your child's sticker chart or may feel like you just don't have the energy to make your child upset by taking away a videogame as a punishment. Strong emotions may also get in the way of maintaining consistency with rewards and punishments. For example, you may neglect to give your child a reward for using Emotion Detective skills before bed because you are still feeling frustrated about a misbehavior that occurred earlier in the day, or you may avoid placing your child in time out because you are feeling too stressed to listen to your child cry or protest. Some parents may also feel guilty for punishing their child, even though they know that their child has misbehaved and understand the importance of consistent punishment for changing their child's behavior. It is important for you to consider factors that may interfere with your own ability to consistently reinforce or discipline your child so that you can make a plan for how to be consistent when these barriers do arise.

Opposite Parenting Behavior: Consistent Discipline/Praise

Now that you have begun to understand the problems with inconsistent reinforcement and discipline, as well as personal factors that might interfere with your own consistency, let's discuss some strategies for helping you to increase consistency in managing your child's emotions and behaviors. The key to creating and implementing effective reinforcement systems and discipline at home is to keep expectations and rules simple and limited in number. Your child will likely become easily overwhelmed if he or she is working toward too many things at once or attempting to follow many rules at once. This may lead your child to give up out of frustration or break rules due to forgetfulness. Similarly, when parents have established many expectations and rules, it becomes difficult to remember to consistently reinforce or punish.

1. Decide which behaviors you want to reinforce, keeping in mind the following points:
   - Choose behaviors that your child is not already doing consistently but are within your child's reach.
   - Work on no more than two or three behaviors at one time. When your child has mastered those, you can work on additional behaviors.
   - State the behaviors you want to see clearly and simply.
   - State what you want your child to do, not what you don't want your child to do.

2. Decide on a reward system and explain to your child how that system will function. Examples of reward systems might include:
   - Placing a sticker or drawing a star on a chart each time your child engages in the desired behavior
   - Placing a token or penny in a jar each time your child engages in the desired behavior

3. Decide how many stickers, stars, or tokens your child needs to earn a prize. Choose a number that is neither too low nor too high. Use the *Rewards List* you and your child created in Session 2 to plan the rewards your child can earn.

4. When your child engages in a desired behavior, reinforce him or her as soon as possible by placing a sticker on the chart or token in the jar.

5. Once your child has been consistently engaging in a desired behavior for several weeks, you can choose a new behavior to work on and begin to reinforce the old one less consistently.

Figure 14.1

Guidelines for Creating a Reinforcement System at Home

On Figure 14.1: *Guidelines for Creating a Reinforcement System at Home* and Figure 14.2: *Guidelines for Creating an Effective Behavior Management System at Home*, you will find some guidelines for how to create and implement effective reinforcement and behavior management systems at home. As you read through these guidelines, consider whether your own methods of reinforcement and discipline conform to them, as well as how you might implement these guidelines in your household.

1. **House rules** are rules that everyone in your household must follow, without exception. House rules should be rules where, if your child were to break them, you would not hesitate to implement a consequence. Parents often choose to create house rules around behaviors like aggression or defiance. When creating house rules, we recommend following these guidelines:

- If you have no house rules currently in place, we recommend beginning with ONE clear house rule. In general, you should avoid introducing more than one or two house rules at a time.
- Clearly explain the house rule to your child, using language that he or she can easily understand.
- Decide what the consequence will be for breaking the house rule. Examples of consequences often used by parents include time out, removal of screen time, or removal of desired activities. Clearly explain the consequence for breaking the rule to your child.
- If your child breaks a house rule, immediately follow through with the stated consequence. This teaches your child that you are serious about the house rule!

2. Parents often *ask* their child to do something rather than *tell* their child to do something, and then subsequently are surprised when their child does not comply. When it is important that your child do something, be sure to use an **effective command** rather than a question. Following are five rules for giving effective commands:

- Gain your child's attention.
  - "Emily, please look at me."
- Once you have your child's attention, use a firm (but not angry) voice requesting your child to do something.
- Issue only one simple command at a time, and allow a brief period of time for your child to comply with the rule.
  - "Emily, turn off the computer."
- If your child complies, reinforce him or her with praise or a reward.
- If your child does not comply, issue the command again.
- If your child still does not comply, a consequence may be given.
  - "Emily, if you don't turn off the computer you will lose screen time for the evening."

3. Although we emphasize the use of positive reinforcement in this treatment, negative punishment (also known as **response cost** procedures) may be used if your child is disobedient or does not comply with a request. As a reminder, negative punishment involves taking a desired activity or item away from your child when your child misbehaves. When using negative punishment or response cost, the following guidelines may be helpful:

- Be sure that you have gained your child's attention, clearly stated a command, and given a warning before implementing response cost procedures.
- State how long you are removing the privilege before removing it. Typically, the time frame should be relatively brief (e.g., one day) so that your child does not feel discouraged.
- Return the privilege to your child exactly when you say you will—not earlier or later.

Figure 14.2

Guidelines for Creating an Effective Behavior Management System at Home

Worksheet 14.1: L for Parents

Our emotions are directly related to our interpretations of any given situation. Strong emotions can make us and our children think in ways that are unrealistic or unhelpful, leading to more feelings of anxiety, sadness, or anger. We call these unhelpful patterns "thinking traps" because they get us stuck in one way of thinking about a situation.

Psychic Suki

Mind Reading: Believing you know what others are thinking without considering other, more likely, possibilities.

Example: You think that your boss believes you're incompetent, even though you've always received good performance reviews.

Your Examples: _____

_____

_____

Jumping Jack

Jumping to Conclusions: Thinking that the chances of something happening are much greater than they actually are.

Example: You think that there is a 90% chance that your plane is going to crash (when the real chance is more like 0.00002%).

Your Examples: _____

_____

_____

Disaster Darrell

Thinking the Worst: Telling yourself that the very worst is happening or is going to happen, without thinking of other, less negative ways the situation could turn out.

Example: Your child is late walking home from school, so you think he or she may have been kidnapped.

Your Examples: _____

_____

_____

Negative Nina

Ignoring the Positive: Telling yourself that your achievements or successes "don't count" and that you just "got lucky." Always focusing on the negative rather than the positive.

Example: You always attend your child's school events and activities, but you can't stop thinking about the soccer game you missed last week due to a work emergency.

Your Examples: _____

_____

_____

Worksheet 14.2: Understanding Learned Behaviors

Your child's behavior may seem quite mysterious, but children learn to use some behaviors more and some less based on the consequences for that behavior. Children learn to do more of a certain behavior when they are rewarded or reinforced for it, and less when they are punished for it. Think about how you reinforce and punish your child.

Positive Reinforcement

What It Is: Providing something your child likes (for example, praise, attention, rewards) for behaviors that you would like to see again.

Example: Putting a sticker on your child's sticker chart when he or she helps with chores in the evening.

Your Example: _____

_____

_____

Negative Reinforcement

What It Is: Introducing something that your child does NOT like and then taking it away when your child engages in a desired behavior.

Example: Yelling at your child until she sits down at the dinner table like she was asked.

Your Example: _____

_____

_____

Positive Punishment

What It Is: Introducing something that your child does NOT like after your child engages in an unwanted behavior.

Example: Making your child help clean his classroom after talking back to the teacher.

Your Example: _____

_____

_____

Negative Punishment

What It Is: Removing something that your child likes after your child engages in an unwanted behavior.

Example: Taking away your child's screen time for starting a fight with her sibling.

Your Examples: _____

_____

_____

CHAPTER 15

Use Detective Thinking and Problem Solving for Parents

(Sessions 6 and 7 for Parents)

- To understand the purpose of Detective Thinking
- To learn how to use the steps of Detective Thinking to gather evidence for emotional thoughts
- To learn about the emotional parenting behaviors of overcontrol and overprotection
- To consider ways of practicing the opposite parenting behavior of healthy independence-granting

Thinking Like a Detective

Try to recall a time when you were feeling pessimistic or negative about something in your life. Maybe you were having difficulty adjusting to a new supervisor's style at work, feeling upset that your child wasn't accepted into the school you wanted her or him to attend, or feeling anxious about an upcoming move or change. In situations like these, where something isn't going the way we might have wanted, changing our perspective or outlook can be quite difficult. Adding to this difficulty, we often get messages that we need to "look on the bright side," "celebrate the positive," or "make lemonade out of lemons." You may have even said something to this effect to your child when he or she was feeling down, negative, or pessimistic about an upcoming situation or event. These common phrases communicate the message that changing our thinking about a situation should be easy, when in reality it is anything but—especially when strong emotions are affecting our thoughts.

For the past week, you and your child have practiced identifying times when your child gets stuck in a **thinking trap**. By now, it is probably easier to recognize when your child is *thinking the worst, mind reading, jumping to conclusions,* or *ignoring the positive.* Now that you both recognize that your child may be thinking about situations in unhelpful or unrealistic ways that encourage strong emotions, what do you do about it? In this session, you and your child will learn a step-by-step process for evaluating thinking traps and considering what else might be true. We call this process **Detective Thinking** because we want to encourage your child to view his or her thoughts like a detective might—as a guess that can be tested against the evidence.

It is important for you and your child to know that Detective Thinking is not all about thinking positively or looking on the bright side. For many people, thinking positively just doesn't work (as you may have found). Many situations that make your child anxious, sad, fearful, or angry are in fact not positive or working out well. Asking your child to think of them as such would likely feel fake, inauthentic, or hopelessly difficult. Rather, Detective Thinking is a skill for teaching your child to think flexibly about situations in which strong emotions would typically cause your child to make *snap judgments*, without considering all the evidence. We want your child to examine the evidence for his or her original thought and *think about what else could be true* in order to arrive at a more realistic, accurate, or helpful perspective on the situation.

Detective Thinking Step by Step

In this treatment, we refer to the steps of Detective Thinking as the **Stop, Slow, Go** steps. "Stop, Slow, Go" describes what your child is doing when he or she is practicing Detective Thinking and provides an easy way to remember each of the steps.

Detective Thinking begins with the **Stop** step because, even before your child enters an emotional situation, we want him or her to stop and identify the thought that is contributing to the strong emotion. We often act on emotional thoughts without even realizing we are having them or taking for granted that they are facts. This can lead to unhelpful emotional behaviors. In the Stop step, your child is identifying the situation, the specific emotional thought he or she is having about that situation, and how likely he or she believes it to be true.

We call the second step of Detective Thinking the **Slow** step because we want your child to learn to slow down and really take a look at the evidence for his or her thought. This can be difficult to do, as the job of emotions is to get us to act quickly, without taking much time to think about our interpretations of a situation. Remember that emotions are natural and helpful in true alarm situations, where spending too much time thinking about what to do can put us in danger or prevent us from getting what we need. In the Slow step, your child will be asking himself or herself a set of detective questions that will help him or her consider what else could be true about the situation.

In the third step—the **Go** step—your child will be re-evaluating the likelihood that the original thought will come true, based on the new evidence gathered, and coming up with a more helpful or realistic coping thought. We call this step the Go step because we want your child to proceed with the situation only after he or she has come up with a new, more accurate thought based on the evidence.

The *U for Parents* worksheet (Worksheet 15.1, at the end of this session) provides a step-by-step guide for practicing Detective Thinking. This worksheet looks exactly the same as the one your child will be using during this session and over the next week to practice Detective Thinking for the home learning assignment. We have provided several copies of this worksheet for you so that you can practice Detective Thinking for some of your own emotional thoughts, in addition to your child's. Detective Thinking can be a difficult skill to practice, and using it for your own emotional thoughts will help you develop empathy for your child when he or she is struggling with this skill—one of our opposite parenting behaviors. Your group leaders may also assign you this worksheet as a home learning exercise.

As we mentioned earlier, our emotions are trying to get us to act quickly, without spending too much time thinking about what's happening in a situation or what we should do about it. For this reason, using Detective Thinking when we are in the height of a strong emotion can often be very difficult! *The best time to use Detective Thinking is actually before we enter a situation likely to bring up feelings of anxiety, sadness, anger, or some other emotion.* Changing the way we think about an emotional situation *before* we even encounter it can help reduce the intensity of our emotions when we are in the situation, allow us to identify skills for coping with the situation ahead of time, and increase the likelihood that we will actually be able to use those skills. However, using Detective Thinking ahead of time does require some planning. At the end of this session, you will complete an activity with your child that involves identifying upcoming emotional situations for which your child would benefit from using Detective Thinking ahead of time.

Emotional Parenting Behavior: Overcontrol and Overprotection

As a parent, you have a natural and helpful impulse to care for your child and protect him or her from dangerous situations. These are things you have been doing for your child since the day he or she was born. In fact, your body even releases certain chemicals when you behave in a caring and protective way toward your child, which is our body's way of positively reinforcing our caretaking efforts. Our biology, emotional responses, and society all work together to promote these protective behaviors, and they are the reason why your child has survived and thrived until now!

The downside of these protective impulses, however, is that they often appear during false-alarm situations, when your child is showing distress but not really in any danger or in high need of your protection or caretaking. When this occurs, we call it **overcontrol** or **overprotection** because you are attempting to control situations your child could navigate on his or her own or protect your child from situations in which he or she does not actually need to be protected. In other words, these situations are distressing for your child, but they are not ones that your child needs to be protected from experiencing. When parents are overcontrolling, they might schedule out their child's entire weekend to make sure he doesn't get too bored or depressed, or they might finish a school project for their child so that she can get the best grade possible. When parents are overprotective, they might talk to their daughter's teacher about an assignment for her because she is too nervous to ask questions, or they might pull their son out of soccer because he is chronically frustrated with his performance or there is a peer on the team who makes him angry and frustrated. When your natural protective urges lead to these types of behaviors, your child might feel better immediately because you are protecting him or her from something that brings up strong emotions. In turn, you may feel better because you are helping your child avoid potentially upsetting situations.

However, just like with our other emotional parenting behaviors, overcontrol and overprotection end up keeping your child stuck in unhelpful cycles of emotional behaviors in the long term. Why does this happen? First, when you step in to control or protect your child from a situation, your child gets the message that there is something about the situation to be feared or avoided. Otherwise, why would Mom or Dad be stepping in? This belief helps maintain your child's fear and distress related to the situation. Second, overcontrolling or overprotective parenting behaviors can reduce your child's feelings of self-efficacy over time. **Self-efficacy** refers your child's belief that he or she is capable of successfully and independently coping with difficult situations or solving challenging problems. Our sense of self-efficacy comes from our repeated experience of facing and learning to cope with these situations or problems. When we prevent our children from gaining these experiences by unnecessarily protecting them, solving problems for them, or controlling situations, we limit their ability to develop this sense of self-efficacy. Finally, overcontrolling and overprotective parenting behaviors keep children stuck in their own cycles of problematic emotional behaviors. Your child may continue to avoid or withdraw from emotional situations because your child knows that you will allow him or her to do so or that you will take care of these situations for your child.

Opposite Parenting Behavior: Healthy Independence-Granting

One important goal of this treatment is to increase your child's confidence in his or her ability to approach and cope with situations that elicit strong emotions or that are difficult for other reasons. You can help your child build confidence and develop better coping skills by gradually beginning to grant him or her more independence in situations you may have previously attempted to control for your child or protect your child from. You should know that, when you first begin to grant your child more independence in these types of situations, he or she may experience a temporary increase in distress. Your child's emotions and behaviors may escalate because he or she is trying to get your attention so that you will step in to protect him or her or control the situation like you have in the past. If you are prepared for this potential escalation, you will be better able to empathize with your child but remain firm in your expectation that he or she will attempt to approach the situation independently.

When you first begin to grant your child more independence, it is important to do so gradually in order to minimize distress and increase your child's likelihood of achieving success. One way of gradually promoting more independent behavior and coping is by **shaping**. Shaping is a helpful parenting strategy to use when you want your child to be able to perform a behavior independently, but you know that he or she will probably not be able to perform the behavior successfully on the first try or all at once. You can use shaping in this type of situation to reward your child whenever he or she successively approximates or gets one step closer to performing the desired behavior. For example, if you have always arranged playdates for your child, calling a friend to invite him over to play may be very difficult for your child to do independently. You may wish to start by praising or rewarding your child's attempts to find out the friend's number, then praise your child for calling or texting the friend to say "hello," and then later for calling the friend to ask about his plans for the weekend.

Over the next week, you will be using Worksheet 15.2: *Encouraging Independent Behaviors* to identify three tasks or situations that you would like to encourage your child to begin approaching more independently. Although these may be tasks or situations that elicit strong emotions for your child, they need not be; they may be tasks like getting ready for school independently in the morning or independently making an afternoon snack. Once you have identified three situations or tasks, choose one to focus on this week. Indicate how you will shape this behavior, as well as rewards or reinforcements you will provide each time your child is able to successively approximate the behavior.

Just as the skills your child is learning in this treatment, like Detective Thinking, can be applied to many different emotions, the opposite parenting behaviors you are learning in this treatment can be applied to many different types of emotional situations. You have learned previously that you can use reinforcement to encourage good behavior and use of Emotion Detective skills to manage emotions more effectively. You have also learned that by ignoring minor misbehavior or emotional displays (e.g., by not reinforcing them with attention), you can decrease these unwanted behaviors. **Positive reinforcement**, **planned ignoring**, and their combination can also be used to encourage independent behaviors in your child. Take a look at Figure 15.1 to see how to do this.

1. **Reinforce** your child's attempts to independently use Emotion Detective skills, solve problems, or approach difficult situations. Just like with reinforcing other behaviors, you may do this using praise, attention, or small rewards. Here are some tips for using reinforcement to encourage independence:
   - Reinforce independent behaviors, regardless of the outcome. For example:
     - Reinforce your child for trying to use a detective skill, even if your child is still anxious or upset.
     - Reinforce your child for creating a schedule to complete school assignments, even if he or she doesn't get everything done.
     - Reinforce your child for getting dressed independently, even if he or she doesn't choose clothes warm enough for the weather.
   - Reinforce your child as soon as possible after he or she completes the independent behavior.
   - Make sure the reinforcement you choose is actually rewarding to your child. For example, many anxious children would feel embarrassed if a parent praised them in front of peers, so praise wouldn't be reinforcing in this context.

2. Practice **planned ignoring** of minor displays of distress and requests for help, particularly in situations where you know your child is capable of performing the independent behavior. If you actively choose not to attend to or reinforce distress or requests for help, these behaviors will gradually cease.

3. Combine positive reinforcement and planned ignoring by **differentially reinforcing** the desired behavior. Even if your child is behaving inappropriately in a situation, you can still reinforce aspects of her or his behavior that will help develop independence. Examples of this include:
   - Reinforcing your child for walking toward the car even though she is whining about having to attend a birthday party
   - Reinforcing your child for continuing to complete homework independently even though he keeps mentioning how boring it is

Figure 15.1

Using Reinforcement to Encourage Independent Behaviors

Worksheet 15.1: U for Parents

When your child gets stuck in a thinking trap, there are Emotion Detective skills your child can use to get out of it. **Detective thinking** is a step-by-step process your child is learning to evaluate emotional thoughts the way a detective might—as guesses to be tested against the evidence. Follow the steps below to identify and gather evidence for either one of your own emotional thoughts **or** one of your child's.

Steps		Answers
What is the situation?		
What is the thought?		
Best guess about what is happening	How likely is it to happen? (0–100%)	
	What is the thinking trap?	
	What's happened in the past? Have I coped with this situation before?	
Clues	Am I 100% sure that my emotional thought is true?	
	What else could be true?	
	Is there anything good about this situation?	
	If my emotional thought is true, can I cope with it?	
Check your best guess	How likely is it to happen? (0–100%)	
What are my coping thoughts?		

Steps			Answers
What is the situation?			
What is the thought?			
Best guess about what is happening	How likely is it to happen? (0–100%)		
	What is the thinking trap?		
	What's happened in the past? Have I coped with this situation before?		
	Am I 100% sure that my emotional thought is true?		
Clues	What else could be true?		
	Is there anything good about this situation?		
	If my emotional thought is true, can I cope with it?		
Check your best guess	How likely is it to happen? (0–100%)		
What are my coping thoughts?			

Steps			Answers
What is the situation?			
What is the thought?			
Best guess about what is happening	How likely is it to happen? (0–100%)		
	What is the thinking trap?		
	What's happened in the past? Have I coped with this situation before?		
Clues	Am I 100% sure that my emotional thought is true?		
	What else could be true?		
	Is there anything good about this situation?		
	If my emotional thought is true, can I cope with it?		
Check your best guess	How likely is it to happen? (0–100%)		
What are my coping thoughts?			

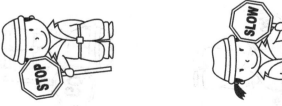

Worksheet 15.2: Encouraging Independent Behaviors

Parents have a natural and helpful impulse to protect and care for their children. However, this impulse can result in overcontrolling or overprotective parenting if we act on it in false alarm situations when our children are not actually in danger or in need of our help. Over the next week, you will begin practicing the opposite parenting behavior, which is healthy independence-granting. To start, identify in the space below, three tasks or situations that you believe your child could be approaching more independently.

Three things my child could be doing more independently are:

1. _____

2. _____

3. _____

Choose one of the behaviors that you have identified above to work on during the next week. In the spaces below, write 3–5 ways to shape this behavior, as well as the reinforcement you will provide when your child completes each approximation or step.

The one behavior that my child will work on performing independently this week is:

_____

Here are the steps toward that behavior I will reinforce this week, and how I will reinforce them:

Step/Approximation	Reinforcement
_____	_____
_____	_____
_____	_____
_____	_____
_____	_____

- To identify the differences between Detective Thinking and Problem Solving—two Emotion Detective skills
- To learn the steps of Problem Solving
- To learn how to help your child apply Problem Solving to conflicts with other people
- To learn how to promote independent use of Detective Thinking and Problem Solving skills at home

Two Emotion Detective Skills: Problem Solving and Detective Thinking

So far in the "U" section of treatment, your child has begun learning some Emotion Detective skills for thinking more helpfully and more flexibly about situations that bring up strong emotions. In the previous session, we focused on helping your child learn to think more flexibly about his or her first thought in emotional situations and treat it as a hypothesis or guess to be tested against the evidence. This skill, which you and your child have hopefully started to practice at home, is called Detective Thinking. **Detective Thinking** is a **secondary control** strategy because it is helpful for times when either the situation is not the real problem or the situation cannot be controlled. Even though your child cannot control the situation, your child can learn to adjust how he or she is thinking about it. The Emotion Detective skill you and your child will be learning today—**Problem Solving**—is sometimes called a **primary control** strategy because it is useful when the situation itself is the problem and your child may be able to do something about it.

To illustrate this, first imagine that your child has been preparing for a big presentation in class on the extinction of the dinosaurs. Your child carefully wrote down the assignment, spoke with the teacher to make sure he or she understood it clearly, started early, and has been practicing for the last couple days. It is clear to you that your child is well prepared, but the morning of the presentation your child begins to worry that he or she did the presentation incorrectly and will get a bad grade. Your child becomes so nervous that he or she asks to stay home from school.

Now imagine your child is in the same situation of having to give a presentation today about the extinction of the dinosaurs, but in this case he or she didn't check in with the teacher ahead of time about the assignment. When your child's friend comes over to walk to school with him or her, the friend tells your child that the presentation isn't supposed to be about the extinction of the dinosaurs at all! Rather, it is supposed to be a detailed presentation about the diet, habitat, and behavior of your child's favorite dinosaur. Your child immediately begins to worry that he or she did the presentation incorrectly and will get a bad grade. Once again, your child asks to stay home from school.

In which of these situations do you think Detective Thinking would be most helpful, and in which do you think Problem Solving would be most helpful? Although it may be possible to use both skills in both situations, Detective Thinking would likely be most helpful in the first situation because your child's thoughts about the situation are the biggest problem. Your child has clearly understood the assignment and is well prepared, so your child's thoughts about having done the presentation incorrectly and receiving a bad grade are likely a thinking trap (perhaps Disaster Darrell, for example). In contrast, in the second situation, your child's thoughts may not be all that inaccurate. Your child has good evidence that he or she *did* do the assignment incorrectly (although a truly bad grade may still be unlikely). Because the situation—having misunderstood an assignment and done it incorrectly—is the main problem here, Problem Solving is likely the best Emotion Detective skill to use. The goal of both skills is to help your child think more flexibly about interpretations of emotional situations or possible solutions to emotional situations, respectively. Hopefully, use of these skills would help your child make it to school!

Problem Solving Step by Step

Problem Solving is a skill that both you and your child have likely practiced before in some fashion, without even realizing you were using it. When we encounter problems that bring up strong emotions like fear, sadness, or anger, we often get stuck in the same rigid ways of solving those problems over and over again. This makes sense if you think back to what we said in the last two sessions about the impact of emotions on flexible thinking. Our emotions are often trying to get us to think quickly so that we can escape dangerous situations or get help right away. This means that, when we face a problem that brings up strong emotions, we often act on the first solution we think of without considering other possible solutions. The problem is that our first solution is not always the most helpful one in the long term. The more we choose the same types of solutions over and over, the more we get stuck in them and the less we think of other types of solutions. The purpose of using Problem Solving

1. Define the problem

What: State the problem as simply, concretely, and specifically as possible.

Why: Your child can't solve a problem without knowing exactly what the problem is. How your child states the problem will influence the kinds of solutions he or she comes up with.

2. Brainstorm solutions

What: Encourage your child to come up with as many solutions as possible, even silly ones or ones your child doesn't think will work.

Why: Children often judge solutions before even really considering them. We want to promote flexible thinking by encouraging you to just brainstorm, without judging yet.

3. List the pros and cons for each solution

What: Now it's time to evaluate! Help your child weigh the merits of hers or his solutions by considering the good and bad things about each one.

Why: Considering each solution carefully helps your child to see advantages of a solution he or she might have immediately dismissed, and disadvantages of a solution your child might have otherwise chosen right away.

4. Pick a solution and try it out!

What: Based on the pros and cons list, help your child choose a solution and try it out. This will likely be a solution with more pros than cons or clear pros that outweigh any cons.

Why: Now that your child has evaluated each solution systematically, your child has enough information and evidence to choose wisely, without simply acting on emotions.

5. If needed, go through the Problem Solving steps again

What: Check in with your child about how the first solution worked. If it didn't work, your child may need to pick a different one or modify the solution he or she tried out.

Why: Even after going through the Problem Solving steps, the solution your child chooses may not work. If this happens, it is a good opportunity to talk with your child about perseverance and trying something until it works.

Figure 15.2

Problem-Solving Steps

is to learn to think more flexibly about solving problems so that we can choose the most helpful solutions.

Problem Solving is a step-by-step process, and it is important for your child to learn and practice all five Problem Solving steps in order for the skill to be effective. Review Figure 15.2 to learn more about each of these steps and some important tips for how to use them with your child.

Just like with the other Emotion Detective skills your child has been learning, Problem Solving can be helpful for adults too. Unfortunately, we all have many problems, and we all have a tendency to get stuck in the same ways of solving them without thinking flexibly about other possible solutions. During this session, your group leaders may walk you through the steps of Problem Solving using some typical types of problems that arise for adults in their day-to-day lives (see Worksheet 15.3: *Problem-Solving Steps Practice*). We also encourage you to consider practicing Problem Solving at home during the week for one of your own problems to get additional practice with this skill.

Applying Problem Solving to Conflicts with Other People

Children who struggle with strong emotions may have more conflicts and other interpersonal challenges with friends, family, teachers, or other adults in their lives than children who do not struggle with strong emotions. There may be several reasons for this. First, conflicts and challenges with other people can certainly *cause* strong emotions, as you probably know all too well from your own experiences. Second, experiencing strong emotions may lead to emotional behaviors like avoidance, withdrawal, and aggression, which can certainly cause problems in your child's relationships with others. Finally, children who struggle with strong emotions may lack effective skills for dealing with others as a result of frequent use of emotional behaviors over time. They may not have good skills for managing conflicts, initiating conversations, advocating for themselves, or getting others to understand their point of view.

The good news is that Problem Solving is an Emotion Detective skill your child can use to plan for these types of challenging situations with other people and choose more effective solutions. Here are some examples of interpersonal situations in which children with strong emotions may benefit from using Problem Solving:

■ Children with anxiety may struggle to stick up for themselves when being bullied or taken advantage of by a friend.

- Children with depression may need to figure out how to repair friendships if they have been isolating or withdrawing from their friends.
- Children who struggle with anger may get into fights with friends or say things they later regret.
- Children with anxiety may have difficulty making new friends after switching schools.
- Children with depression may fail to turn in assignments due to fatigue or lack of motivation, leading to poor grades or problems with teachers.
- Children who struggle with siblings may have difficulty playing calmly with them without getting into fights or arguments.

Think about the types of situations with other people *your* child tends to struggle with. When these problems arise, suggest that he or she use the problem-solving steps to figure out what to do. You may need to initially guide your child through the steps, suggest additional solutions if your child sees limited possibilities, and point out additional pros and cons that your child may miss. As you help your child brainstorm and weigh the pros and cons of each solution, also consider her or his current skills and capabilities. For example, a very socially anxious child starting a new school may have great difficulty asking to join a game or sitting at a table with completely unfamiliar peers during lunch. If your child is thinking of many solutions that appear discrepant with his or her current skill level, you may need to guide your child toward some solutions that are more realistic or feasible.

Promoting Independence with Detective Thinking and Problem Solving

During the last session, we spent some time discussing the emotional parenting behaviors of overcontrol and overprotection, as well as their opposite parenting behavior of healthy independence-granting. Since then, you have begun to identify behaviors that your child could be performing more independently, as well as ways to shape the behaviors though successive approximations (steps) and use of rewards. Over the next few weeks, you should continue to use shaping to promote these independent behaviors in your child. In addition, we also want you to begin applying these principles to the Emotion Detective skills your child has been learning in the "U" section of this treatment—Detective Thinking and Problem Solving—so that he or she can begin to use these skills more independently.

When children experience strong emotions, they often ask for reassurance from their parents or other adults, or they attempt to recruit parents or others to solve problems for them. As we have discussed, parents have a natural impulse to protect and take care of their children, so parents often step in to provide reassurance or fix problems without hesitation. This often makes parents feel helpful and effective, and it may also seem to temporarily reduce their child's distress. However, you may have guessed by now that providing too much reassurance or stepping in to solve challenging problems for your child represents another form of overprotection or overcontrol. The more reassurance you provide your child, the more he or she becomes dependent upon your reassurance and the less able he or she becomes to independently evaluate whether the feared outcome is realistic. Reassurance-seeking becomes an emotional behavior your child turns to whenever he or she feels distressed, and some children may even come to believe that a situation will *only* turn out okay if their parent reassures them that it will. Similarly, when parents step in to solve problems for their children, children become less flexible and effective in solving their own problems and lose confidence in their ability to do so.

Fortunately, your child now has two new Emotion Detective skills to use instead of seeking the reassurance of getting you to solve his or her problems—Detective Thinking and Problem Solving. Over the next week, your job is to promote more independent use of these skills by encouraging your child to practice Detective Thinking whenever he or she begins to seek excessive reassurance, and by encouraging your child to practice Problem Solving whenever he or she seems stuck and is asking you to solve a problem for him or her. When deciding how to promote independent use of these skills, think about what your child is currently capable of. Some children pick up these skills quickly and enjoy using them; for these children, a prompt such as "remember your Detective Thinking" or "why don't you go through the Problem Solving steps for this situation?" may be enough. Sometimes responding to requests for reassurance with something as brief as "What do you think (about that situation)?" can work for some children. Other children may require more shaping and may need you to walk them through each step of Detective Thinking or Problem Solving in the beginning until they become more comfortable using these skills.

Your home learning assignment for this session is to use *Shaping Detective Thinking and Problem Solving at Home* (Worksheet 15.4) to begin to practice shaping your child's use of these Emotion Detective skills at home. When your child is thinking unrealistically or unhelpfully about a situation this week or encounters a problem, help him or her to complete the Detective Thinking or Problem Solving steps, respectively. Try to strike a balance between helping your child recall and practice the steps while encouraging him or her to do so independently as much as possible. There are columns on this worksheet for you to indicate where your child currently needs your help with these skills, as well as how you plan to promote more independence the next time based on your experiences this week. Don't forget to give your child a small reward for practicing each skill!

Worksheet 15.3: Problem Solving Steps Practice

Practice applying the Problem Solving steps you just learned to a problem situation from your own life that is making you feel stuck. Practicing these steps with your own problems will allow you to more effectively help your child practice this important detective skill, and it will hopefully help you to solve your own problem as well.

1. Define the problem

2. Brainstorm solutions

1. _____

2. _____

3. _____

4. _____

5. _____

3. List the pros and cons for each solution

Solutions	Pros	Cons
1.	_____	_____
2.	_____	_____
3.	_____	_____
4.	_____	_____
5.	_____	_____

4. Pick a solution and try it out!
My solution is:

1. Define the problem

2. Brainstorm solutions

1. _____

2. _____

3. _____

4. _____

5. _____

3. List the pros and cons for each solution

Solutions	Pros	Cons
1.	_____	_____
2.	_____	_____
3.	_____	_____
4.	_____	_____
5.	_____	_____

4. Pick a solution and try it out!

My solution is:

Worksheet 15.4: Shaping Detective Thinking and Problem Solving at Home

Detective Thinking and Problem Solving are incredibly helpful—and sometimes difficult—skills for children to learn. Last week, you began to use shaping to break independent behaviors you would like to see from your child into steps or successive approximations. This week, you will practice shaping Detective Thinking and Problem Solving. We have already broken these skills down into steps for you. For each step, indicate whether your child was able to complete the step independently or whether your child required you to help shape the step. Completing this worksheet will help you figure out where your child is with these skills so that you can gradually provide less help over time and grant more independence to your child. Also, don't forget to reward your child for practicing the skill—an important part of shaping!

Shaping Detective Thinking		
Step	**Did my child require my assistance?**	**How I can help my child complete this step more independently next time**
1. Remembering to use Detective Thinking	Y/N	
2. Remembering "Stop, Slow, Go"	Y/N	
3. Identifying the situation and unhelpful thought	Y/N	
4. Identifying the thinking trap	Y/N	
5. Remembering to ask detective questions	Y/N	
6. Coming up with a new and more realistic thought, based on evidence	Y/N	
Reward I Gave My Child:		

Shaping Problem Solving		
Step	**Did my child require my assistance?**	**How I can help my child complete this step more independently next time**
1. Remembering to use Problem Solving	Y/N	
2. Remembering the five steps of Problem Solving	Y/N	
3. Identifying the problem	Y/N	
4. Brainstorming and evaluating solutions	Y/N	
5. Choosing a solution	Y/N	
6. Remembering to try out the solution	Y/N	
Reward I Gave My Child:		

CHAPTER 16

Experience My Emotions for Parents

(Sessions 8–14 for Parents)

SESSION 8 GOALS

- To understand the importance of experiencing emotions rather than avoiding or suppressing them
- To learn about and practice present-moment awareness
- To learn about and practice nonjudgmental awareness
- To begin to create an *Emotional Behaviors Form—Parent Version* in preparation for upcoming exposures

Why Experience Emotions?

Welcome to the E section of treatment: "Experience My Emotions." The E skill is the longest of all the CLUES skills (seven sessions long!), and its length reflects its fundamental importance to this treatment. In this section of treatment, your child will begin to approach and experience situations that bring up strong emotions, without using avoidance or other emotional behaviors to lessen or escape from the emotion. In our experience, many parents notice that the fastest and most dramatic gains occur during this section of treatment. The E section of treatment also gives your child many opportunities to put all of the C, L, and U skills he or she has been learning into action in real-life situations when strong emotions come up.

When experiencing strong emotions in the past, your child has likely tried very hard to get rid of the emotions (and may have discovered emotional behaviors that are very successful in doing so in the short term!). For example, your child may be very used to avoiding, withdrawing from, lashing out at, suppressing, or ignoring emotions. Although these types of emotional behaviors may result in short-term relief, as we have reviewed before, these emotional behaviors often maintain or even intensify strong emotions in the long term, reinforce problematic cycles of emotional behaviors, and reduce children's sense of self-efficacy in emotional situations.

During the E section of treatment, we will be taking the opposite stance toward strong emotions by encouraging your child to gradually approach and sit with uncomfortable emotions, without doing anything to avoid or suppress them. You should be prepared that this may be very uncomfortable for your child at first, and some children even experience increased symptoms for a limited amount of time as they begin to experience emotions they have been avoiding or ignoring. However, as your child practices experiencing his or her emotions, he or she will begin to learn that strong emotions don't last very long if we let them run their course. As a result, your child will begin to have less distress in response to strong emotion, and the duration and strength of your child's emotional experiences will lessen over time. Your child will also learn to apply the Emotion Detective skills he or she has learned in treatment to manage these strong emotions more effectively.

In this session, your child will learn some general skills for just noticing and being aware of emotions as they come up. During the next session, your child will practice using these skills in session to sit with and experience mild levels of emotional distress. During sessions 10 through 14, your child will apply all of his or her Emotion Detective skills as he or she begins to do activities that involve approaching situations that have previously brought up strong emotions and led to troublesome emotional behaviors, such as avoidance. These activities are called **situational emotional exposures**, and you and your child will be learning much more about these during the next treatment session. For now, let's discuss some skills that will help your child learn to just notice, experience, and stay with emotions until they pass.

Present-Moment Awareness

Have you ever had the experience of arriving somewhere but not recalling anything about the drive over? Of quickly finishing a meal on the go but not feeling at all satisfied? Of attending a training or presentation and, when it's about over, realizing that you weren't paying attention to anything the speaker said? We have all had experiences like these of being completely unaware of the present moment, perhaps caught up in our thoughts about an argument that happened yesterday with our spouse, about all the tasks we need to complete before the end of the day, or perhaps just zoning out. This is sometimes called being on **autopilot**, which refers to going through our daily routines without awareness of what we are doing or how we are doing it.

Being on autopilot a lot of the time and not paying attention to the present moment can have a significant impact upon our mood and our emotions. First, research has shown that being aware of the activity we are currently doing, regardless of what it is, makes us happier than being unaware. Being aware of the present moment also allows us to more accurately identify our current emotions and their intensity. If we don't know what we are feeling and why, we are more likely to act on our emotions without first thinking through the best course of action. The more aware we become of our emotions, the more we see that they naturally ebb and flow on their own and that they will eventually go away without us doing anything about them.

Present-moment awareness is a kind of opposite behavior to being on autopilot. Present-moment awareness involves paying attention to only what is happening right now in the present moment, rather than in the past (which we cannot change) or in the future (which hasn't happened yet). When we practice present-moment awareness, we are noticing the present moment, saying something about it to ourselves, and allowing ourselves to fully experience it. A more thorough description of each of these present-moment awareness skills can be found in Figure 16.1: *Notice It, Say Something About It, Experience It.*

In this session, your child is practicing several exercises to become more aware of the present moment, and you may also do some of these exercises in the parent group session. This coming week, you and your child should continue to practice present-moment awareness (as well as nonjudgmental awareness—discussed below), this time applying these skills to emotions, situations, and experiences that arise naturally during the week. Many children have great difficulty learning these skills, so you may wish to practice them with your child first in non-emotional

Present-moment awareness is a skill that involves purposefully focusing your attention on the sensations, emotions, and experiences occurring right here in the present moment. When we focus on the present moment only, we focus less on worries about the past or future, become more aware of the parts of our current emotional experience, including our thoughts, physical sensations, and behaviors, and learn that emotions come and go and are not dangerous on their own. Present-moment awareness involves taking three steps: noticing what is around or inside of us, saying something to ourselves about our experience, and fully experiencing things in the here and now. Continue reading to learn more about each of these skills and how to practice them with your child.

- **Notice It**

  "Noticing It" involves wordlessly attending to what is inside or around us. Help your child notice what is around him or her, using all five senses, as well as any internal body sensations your child might be experiencing. Encourage your child to just notice, without putting words to his or her experiences.

- **Say Something About It**

  "Saying Something About It" involves stating the facts of our external and internal experiences without judgment. Now encourage your child to say something about what he or she noticed in as much detail as possible. Help your child say something about what colors, textures, tastes, temperatures, sensations, or smells he or she noticed. Encourage your child to stick to the facts and just describe what is there, rather than judging internal or external sensations.

- **Experience it**

  "Experiencing It" involves throwing ourselves into the present moment and fully experiencing what is happening in the here and now. Help your child experience the present moment by keeping your child engaged and focused on what he or she is doing and minimizing distractions.

Remember: When practicing present-moment awareness, distracting thoughts or judgments may come up. If this happens, gently bring your child's attention (and your own) back to what is happening in the present moment.

Figure 16.1

Notice It, Say Something About It, Experience It

Table 16.1 Example Non-emotional and Emotional Situations for Awareness Practice

Non-emotional Situations	Emotional Situations
Taking a walk around the neighborhood	Studying for a test
Performing a chore	Losing in a game and feeling frustrated
Riding in the car	Watching a sad or scary television show
Playing a sport or game	Being late for an event or practice
Eating a snack	Practicing an instrument
Playing with a toy	Being unable to play outside due to rain

situations (such as practicing being aware while eating or walking), and then gradually work up to practicing them in emotional situations (practicing being aware when he or she is experiencing a tough emotion). You can find some more examples of both non-emotional and emotional situations in which to help your child practice these forms of awareness in Table 16.1.

Nonjudgmental Awareness

Imagine that a new restaurant just opened in your neighborhood. You run into a friend who just ate at the restaurant the other night. She raves about the restaurant, stating that the food was spectacular, the atmosphere comfortable and relaxing, and the service the best she's had anywhere in a long time. You then run into your neighbor, who also recently went to the new restaurant. In contrast to your friend's review, your neighbor tells you that the food was bland, the atmosphere boring, and the service rude. How would the judgments of each of these friends influence your own experience of the restaurant? Which judgment would convince you to have a meal there, and which would make you want to stay home?

A **judgment** is an evaluation of something's or someone's value or worth. To judge is human—we all make judgments every day, about all kinds of things and situations. You are making a judgment of the morning's traffic if you state that it is "horrible," about your child's performance when you tell him that his test grade was "good," or about your lunch when you say it tastes "gross." Many of the judgments we make on a daily basis are harmless, and even beneficial. If we think in evolutionary terms, judging a piece of rotten fruit or an attacker as "bad" helped keep our ancestors safe. However, judgments can cause problems in some situations, particularly when we judge our emotions and emotional reactions.

Children (and adults) who struggle with strong emotions tend to make more negative judgments about their emotions than other people do. Your child might be making a judgment about his or her emotions if he or she believes that it's wrong to be angry, stupid to cry when feeling upset, or dumb to feel afraid of something that doesn't bother other kids. Such negative judgments about emotions make your child all the more upset when he or she does experience or express emotions, because your child believes that it's not okay to feel that way. Your child may then try even harder to do something to get rid of or avoid the negative emotions attached to those judgments, increasing problematic cycles of emotional behaviors.

Your child will be practicing a skill during this session called **nonjudgmental awareness** that will help him or her take a more neutral, curious, and even kind attitude toward his or her emotional experiences. Nonjudgmental awareness is a type of present-moment awareness that involves noticing and saying something about our emotions in a factual, neutral, and nonjudgmental way. Because judgments often intensify our emotional reactions, practicing nonjudgmental awareness of emotions and emotional situations can help reduce the intensity of strong emotions.

Parents of children with emotional disorders often become frustrated and discouraged by their child's strong emotions and emotional behaviors. Frustration, discouragement, and other feelings can lead parents to make judgments about their child or their child's behaviors. For example, parents might think their child is being "ridiculous" when throwing a tantrum before school, or that their child is being "naughty" for yelling at a sibling. These judgments are completely natural—all parents make them from time to time. However, judgments can increase your frustration and discouragement with your child and lead to some of the emotional parenting behaviors we have discussed during this treatment. Sticking to the facts and simply describing your child's behaviors can increase empathy for your child and reduce the likelihood of engaging in emotional parenting behaviors. For your home learning assignment this week, use

Worksheet 16.1: *Parent Nonjudgmental Awareness Practice at Home* to write down some of your own judgments about your child that arise over the coming week, as well as how you changed those judgments into more neutral statements. Notice how changing your judgments impacts your emotions and thoughts about your child, and write down any changes you notice.

Creating an Emotional Behavior Form—Parent Version

In a couple of weeks, your child will begin to approach emotional situations he or she is currently avoiding, or gradually stop using emotional behaviors in situations that elicit strong emotions. These are called **exposures**—a term you will be learning a lot more about during the next session. Your child will complete exposures both in session and at home each week. To begin to prepare for these exposures, you will need to create a list of different situations that currently bring up strong emotions for your child, such as anger, worry, fear, or sadness, as well as the emotional behaviors your child uses in those situations. You should begin to do this at home this week using the *Emotional Behavior Form—Parent Version* (Form 16.1). Your group leaders or your child's therapist will review this form with you during the next session, and your child's therapist will also work with you and your child next week to add more items to your and your child's *Emotional Behavior Form*.

In preparation for the next session, try to generate at least four or five different situations in which your child experiences strong emotions, including fear, worry, sadness, anger, or others, especially ones where their resultant emotional behaviors (for example, avoiding situations that make them fearful or sad, or fighting with others when they are in situations that make them angry) are not helpful in the long term. For each situation, use the form to indicate the unhelpful emotional behaviors your child exhibits, as well as the intensity or strength of emotion you believe your child experiences (on the emotion thermometer). For now, don't worry about the order of the items on the list—your group leaders and/or your child's therapist will help you begin to develop an order for practicing exposures that makes sense in the next two sessions.

Worksheet 16.1: Parent Nonjudgmental Awareness Practice at Home

As discussed in this chapter, all parents make judgments from time to time about their children. These judgments can lead to parent frustration and discouragement, increasing the likelihood of the parent using emotional parenting behaviors. In the spaces provided below, indicate any judgments that you made about your child's emotions or behaviors this week, as well as how you changed (or could have changed) these judgments into more factual or neutral statements. In the final column on the right, note how changing your judgments into factual statements impacted your emotions and interpretation of your child's emotions or behaviors.

Judgment about My Child's Emotions or Behaviors	Neutral or Factual Statement about My Child's Emotions or Behaviors	How Changing My Judgment Impacted My Emotions and Thoughts about My Child

Form 16.1: Emotional Behavior Form—Parent Version

Use this form to identify and describe situations that cause your child to feel strong emotions, as well as the emotional behaviors your child uses in these situations. Using the Emotion Thermometer below, rate how much uncomfortable *emotion* your child experiences in each situation. When creating this list, think of unhelpful behaviors like avoidance, escape, or other undesired actions (like aggression) that you hope may change during treatment. You and your child can use the last column (Did you work on it?) to see how much progress your child has made on these behaviors over time.

No strong emotion	A little strong emotion	Medium strong emotion	A lot of strong emotion	Very, very strong emotion

0   1   2   3   4   5   6   7   8

Situation	Emotional Behavior	How strong is the emotion (0–8)?	Did you work on it (Y/N)?

■ To learn about situational emotion exposures—a different type of science experiment

■ To learn about your role in helping your child practice exposures at home

■ To learn about the final emotional parenting behavior—excessive modeling of intense emotions and avoidance

■ To learn about the final opposite parenting behavior—healthy emotional modeling

■ To continue to develop your child's *Emotional Behavior Form*

Understanding Situational Emotion Exposures

During the past eight sessions of this treatment, your child has participated in several different types of experiments that involve experiencing an emotion and either (1) doing the opposite of what the emotion told your child to do or (2) just noticing the emotion without doing anything about it. First, in Session 3, your child put on his or her scientist lab coat to see what would happen when he or she practiced doing the opposite of what sadness or boredom wanted your child to do. Then, in Session 4, your child did some experiments to bring on uncomfortable physical sensations and observe what happened to those sensations as a result of just noticing them, without doing anything to get them to go away. Finally, in Session 8, your child learned how to use awareness skills to notice, say something about, and experience his or her emotions in a nonjudgmental way. By participating in these different types of experiments, your child has likely begun to learn that emotions, while sometimes uncomfortable, are not bad or dangerous and will go away even if he or she doesn't act on them.

Each of these experiments has helped to lay the foundation for **situational emotion exposures**—a new type of experiment your child will begin to participate in during the next session. During situational emotion exposures, your child will gradually approach situations that bring up strong emotions—including anxiety, sadness, anger, and others—and stay in the situation without engaging in avoidance or other emotional behaviors. Research has shown that exposures like these are one of the most effective interventions for individuals who struggle with

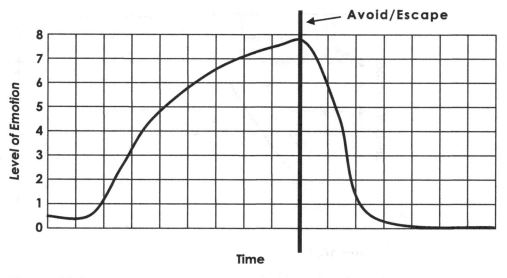

Figure 16.2

Emotion Curve: Avoidance/Escape

strong emotions, and there are at least three different reasons why they work so well.

Think for a moment about what happens when your child encounters a situation that brings up strong emotions. Your child's level of emotion likely starts out low and then quickly increases. If your child is afraid of dogs, for example, he or she might experience something like this if he or she is walking down the street and suddenly a dog begins to approach. Figure 16.2: *Emotion Curve: Avoidance/Escape* illustrates the rapid increase in emotional intensity your child might experience in this situation. The black vertical line shows the point at which your child might engage in an emotional behavior, such as turning around and walking in the opposite direction from the dog. Notice that when your child escapes from the situation, his or her level of emotion quickly goes down.

Now, let's take a look at Figure 16.3: *Emotion Curve: Habituation* to see what would happen if your child didn't avoid the dog or use emotional behaviors in other situations that trigger uncomfortable emotions. Notice that the level of emotion does not decrease as quickly as it did in the previous figure, but it does become less intense over time. By staying in the emotional situation and just allowing the emotion to be there, without engaging in emotional behaviors like walking away, the intensity of the emotion decreases over time. This is called **habituation**, and it is one explanation for why exposures are so effective.

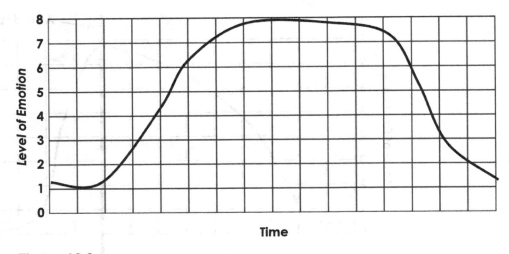

Figure 16.3

Emotion Curve: Habituation

Although habituation often occurs in the manner illustrated in Figure 16.3, it doesn't always and in fact doesn't have to in order for exposures to be effective. Your child's level of strong emotion may not return to "0" the first time he or she completes an exposure, and it may not necessarily even decrease much. This can sometimes be discouraging for children and families, but it doesn't have to be, and it can be a good opportunity for you to reinforce the idea that sometimes we need to practice something over and over before we notice any change or improvement. Figure 16.4: *Emotion Curve: Habituation with Practice* shows that the more your child practices staying in an emotional situation or sticking with an uncomfortable emotion, the less intense the emotion becomes, and it lasts for a shorter period of time. To return to the dog example, the

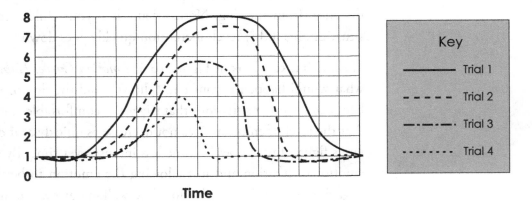

Figure 16.4

Emotion Curve: Habituation with Practice

more your child practices staying around dogs without trying to escape or avoid them, the less afraid your child feels around dogs over time. In other words, even if habituation does not occur during an individual exposure, it often does occur with repeated practice.

As we hinted at earlier, habituation isn't the only (or even necessarily the most important) explanation for why exposures are so effective. As you learned earlier in this treatment, when your child approaches an emotional situation, there is a good chance your child is falling into a thinking trap, such as thinking that the worst will happen (Disaster Darrell) or ignoring the positive aspects of the situation (Negative Nina). If your child continues to avoid or use emotional behaviors in these situations, he or she never has an opportunity to see that the situation is not as bad as he or she thought it would be, or that there may even be positive aspects of the situation. Exposures allow children to test out their unhelpful or unrealistic beliefs about a situation, disconfirm them, and come up with new and more realistic beliefs based on evidence. The more time your child spends around dogs, for example, the less evidence your child has that dogs will attack him or her and the more evidence your child accumulates that most dogs are friendly.

Finally, exposures are so helpful because they teach your child that he or she can tolerate uncomfortable emotions and get through them without doing anything to avoid or lessen them. This is particularly true when habituation does not (or does not fully) occur. Your child becomes much more confident in his or her ability to get through tough emotions, and as a result, those emotions bother your child less over time.

Supporting Your Child's Exposure Practice

Think for a moment about the last time you approached a situation that brought up strong emotions for you—such as feelings of anxiety, fear, sadness, anger, or guilt. Maybe this was an interview for a job you really wanted, an important presentation you had to make at work, or a difficult conversation with your spouse or other loved one. Most likely, it was difficult to approach the situation or engage in the situation without using any emotional behaviors. You may have thought about avoiding the situation entirely, had to talk yourself into approaching the situation or refraining from emotional behaviors once in it, and probably felt quite relieved when it was over. Thinking about your own experience with managing strong emotions can help you develop empathy for your child as he

1. **Help your child to choose which exposure to complete.** The exposure should be neither too easy nor too difficult. An exposure that is about a "3" or "4" out of "8" on the emotion thermometer is a good one to start with.

2. **Help your child plan where and when he or she will complete the exposure.** By definition, exposures may create some temporary distress! As a result, most children will not plan exposures on their own, especially at first. Your child will require your help in planning a time and place for completing the exposure.

3. **Help your child identify what he or she will do during the exposure.** Be as specific and concrete as possible.

4. **Make sure that you gather any necessary materials for the exposure.** Some exposures require you and your child to use special materials, go to a specific place, or interact with certain people. Plan ahead!

5. **Before the exposure, help your child identify the level of his or her emotion and the feared outcome.** Encourage your child to use skills (e.g., Detective Thinking) before beginning the exposure. But be careful not to talk for too long or communicate too much about potential threats in the exposure or provide excessive reassurance about exposures to come.

6. **If your child appears to be struggling to begin the exposure or stick with it, express empathy and encouragement.**

7. **If it becomes apparent that the exposure is too difficult for your child, work with your child to find a way to slightly reduce the difficulty level.** Remember, the goal is for your child to feel successful after the exposure. Because it is sometimes difficult to guess how distressing a situation may be, you may need to adjust the difficulty of the exposure for your child to achieve success. Even small steps forward can be successes!

8. **Encourage your child to compare what he or she thought would happen to what actually did happen (after the exposure ends).** One reason exposures work is that they challenge our beliefs about what will happen in a situation. Highlight the difference between your child's expectations and reality.

9. **Reinforce your child for completing the exposure.** Use praise and/or rewards!

Figure 16.5

Supporting Your Child's Exposures at Home

or she begins situational emotion exposures, which involve approaching situations that bring up uncomfortable emotions again and again.

As a parent you have an important role in supporting your child's exposures and helping him or her be successful. You have already begun to do this by working on your child's *Emotional Behavior Form*, which you will continue to work on during this session with the group leaders and during the next session with your child. Your child will be completing exposures during group sessions 10 through 14 of this treatment, and it is crucial that your child also practice exposures at home. If you recall the emotion curves shown in the previous figures, sometimes exposures must be practiced over and over in order for the intensity of an emotion to decrease. Figure 16.5: *Supporting Your Child's Exposures at Home* contains some helpful suggestions and strategies for maximizing your child's success with at-home exposures. You may wish to refer back to this figure from time to time during the remainder of treatment.

Emotional Parenting Behavior: Excessive Modeling of Intense Emotions and Avoidance

One of the primary means through which humans learn is **modeling**, which means learning a behavior by watching someone else demonstrate or *model* that behavior. Think for a moment about all of the different types of behaviors you have learned through observation. From learning a dance or sport, to learning how to perform duties at work, to learning the behavior that is expected of you in a meeting, modeling influences our behavior on a daily basis. Much of this modeling, especially when it comes to learning norms and expectations, occurs outside of our awareness.

Children typically learn much more information and at a faster pace than do adults, and much of this learning occurs through modeling. Parents tend to be the most influential models for children, including when it comes to emotions. Children learn to express and manage their emotions in part by watching how important people in their lives (particularly parents) express and manage their own emotions. Therefore, as your child begins to approach distressing situations without using emotional behaviors, it is important for you to think about how you typically respond to situations and emotions that you yourself experience. You should know that if you express strong emotions very frequently or inappropriately, or engage in emotional behaviors in front of your child, you may be unintentionally teaching your child to respond to emotions in a similar way. Everyone uses emotional behaviors occasionally, and you are certainly allowed, expected, and encouraged to have your own emotional experiences. However, we also encourage you to think about how you are expressing and managing emotions in front of your child. Just as your child can learn unhelpful ways of coping with emotions through modeling, your child can also learn more helpful, healthier ways of coping by observing you and significant other adults.

Opposite Parenting Behavior: Healthy Emotional Modeling

When you model emotions for your child, keep in mind that the message you ultimately want to communicate is that emotions are normal, natural, and not harmful. Therefore, if you are feeling angry, anxious, or sad, *it's okay to say so*! Chances are your child may notice that something is upsetting you anyway, and if you deny or don't acknowledge it, your child may feel confused. When you discuss how you're feeling with your child, it is helpful for you to identify the trigger (e.g., "I'm feeling sad because a friend from work took a new job and I won't see her at the office anymore"). This helps teach your child to make connections between triggers and his or her own emotions. Try to take a nonjudgmental and accepting stance toward your own emotions around your child by communicating that your own emotions are important and okay. Finally, choose a skill you think would be helpful for managing your own emotions, and model using that skill for your child. For example, in the situation of your coworker taking a new job, you could model Detective Thinking (e.g., "Another way to look at this is that we'll have to make a point to see each other more often outside of work") or doing the opposite of what sadness wants you to do in the situation (e.g., "I think we should watch a funny show together—that will help me feel better").

For your home learning assignment, you will practice modeling emotions in a healthy way around your child. Worksheet 16.2: *Learning Healthy Emotional Modeling* describes three steps for modeling emotions in a healthy manner. Your job is to identify some situations where you tend to express or cope with emotions in an unhelpful manner, and use the steps on the worksheet to change the way you are modeling emotions in front of your child.

Since the last session, you have been working on developing your child's *Emotional Behavior Form—Parent Version* by considering some situations that bring up strong emotions for your child, as well as the intensity of those emotions. You will continue to work on this form during today's session with your group leaders, so that by next week you will have a complete draft of the form. At the end of this session, your child will provide input as well and you will work with your child to integrate your ideas with his or hers to come up with a final form to use in sessions moving forward. As you continue to work on the *Emotional Behavior Form— Parent Version*, here are some questions to consider:

- Do the items on the form reflect the problems and difficulties that brought you and your child to treatment in the first place?
- Are the items on the form specific and concrete?
- Have you included items that range in difficulty (e.g., some low difficulty, some medium difficulty, and some high difficulty)?

We have provided an additional copy of Form 16.2: *Emotional Behavior Form—Parent Version* for you to use as you continue to work on developing your child's form during this session, should you need it.

Worksheet 16.2: Learning Healthy Emotional Modeling

One way children learn to express and manage their emotions is through modeling, or observing how parents and other adults express and manage their own emotions. This means that as a parent, you can teach your child to express and manage emotions differently by changing the way you respond to your own emotions. Review the steps below for modeling emotions in a healthy manner, and consider how you might follow these steps in response to your own emotional triggers.

1. **Label the trigger and the emotion you are experiencing.**
   Why?: Helps your child learn to recognize triggers for emotions and pair emotional experiences with emotion words.
   Example: "Mom is feeling anxious right now because we are late for therapy."

2. **Verbally adopt a nonjudgmental stance to the emotion.**
   Why?: Helps your child to notice and describe emotions objectively without over- reacting to them. Also teaches your child that having emotions is okay!
   Example: "It makes sense that I'm anxious right now because I hate being late. It's okay to feel the way I'm feeling."

3. **Identify and use an appropriate skill or coping strategy for managing the emotion.**
   Why?: Helps your child learn how and when to use Emotion Detective skills.
   Example: "I'm worried that the group leaders will be angry at us. That sounds a lot like Disaster Darrell, so I'm going to use Detective Thinking to come up with a more realistic thought."

Now that you have learned steps for healthy emotional modeling, it is time to put them into practice. Over the next week, identify some situations where you tend to express your emotions in an unhelpful manner and/or use emotional behaviors. Once this week, when you are with your child, practice the steps above for modeling healthy emotion expression and coping instead.

Situation or Trigger	How I Express My Emotions

The situation in which I used healthy emotional modeling was:	
How I labeled the trigger/emotion:	
How I adopted a nonjudgmental stance:	
Emotion Detective skills I modeled:	

Form 16.2: Emotional Behavior Form—Parent Version

Use this form to identify and describe situations that cause your child to feel strong emotions, as well as the emotional behaviors your child uses in these situations. Using the Emotion Thermometer below, rate how much uncomfortable *emotion* your child experiences in each situation. When creating this list, think of unhelpful behaviors like avoidance, escape, or other undesired actions (like aggression) that you hope may change during treatment. You and your child can use the last column (Did you work on it?) to see how much progress your child has made on these behaviors over time.

No strong emotion	A little strong emotion	Medium strong emotion	A lot of strong emotion	Very, very strong emotion

0   1   2   3   4   5   6   7   8

Situation	Emotional Behavior	How strong is the emotion (0–8)?	Did you work on it (Y/N)?

- To learn about applying situational emotion exposure to different types of problem areas
- To learn about safety behaviors and how to reduce your child's use of them
- To identify how to use your opposite parenting behaviors to support your child's exposures
- To learn the purpose of an *Emotion Ladder* for exposures and begin to create one with your child

Applying Exposure to Different Problem Areas

In the previous session, you and your child learned about **situational emotion exposures**, a new type of experiment where we see what happens when we gradually approach and stick with emotional situations without using avoidance or other unhelpful emotional behaviors. To review, researchers and therapists believe that there may be at least four reasons why exposures work so well:

1. your child learns that his or her strong emotions go down by waiting long enough for this to happen;
2. your child learns that his or her strong emotions decrease a little more each time he or she approaches the situation;
3. your child learns that his or her beliefs about the situation are unrealistic or unhelpful and develops new beliefs;
4. your child learns that he or she can tolerate even very strong emotions.

Your child will be getting a chance to put these ideas about exposure to the test in this session, during which he or she will complete a gentle group exposure with the other Emotion Detectives in the group. We begin with a group exposure so that your child can encourage and receive encouragement from the other Emotion Detectives and see that it is okay to experience strong emotions. Then, before the next session, you will help your child complete a situational emotion exposure at home.

Exposures were initially thought of to help children and adults face and overcome their fears or anxieties. However, situational emotion exposures can be applied to almost any type of emotion and can help your child learn to tolerate and cope more effectively with all kinds of emotions, including

Table 16.2 Exposure Examples for Different Problem Areas

Emotion or Problem Area	Exposure
Fear/Anxiety	■ Looking at pictures or watching videos of a feared animal, object, or situation
	■ Observing a feared animal, object, or situation without engaging with it
	■ Touching a feared animal or object or participating in a feared situation
Worry	■ Being exposed to a feared outcome during session (e.g., failing a difficult practice test in session)
	■ Purposely making a minor mistake on a homework assignment and not correcting it
	■ Having to separate from a parent/loved one and not knowing exactly where he or she is
Panic	■ Doing an activity to bring on uncomfortable physical sensations
	■ Approaching objects or staying in situations associated with panic or uncomfortable physical sensations
Obsessions and Compulsions	■ These are generally referred to as *exposure and response prevention* and comprise (1) exposures meant to elicit an intrusive thought and urge to perform a compulsive action (exposure) and (2) practice resisting performing the compulsive action (response prevention). This might be done in the following ways:
	■ Touching something "dirty" or "contaminated" without washing hands
	■ "Messing up" personal items or objects in the room and not fixing or ordering them right away
	■ Thinking about something bad happening (e.g., purposely bringing to mind an intrusive thought) without using a ritual to protect against it
Sadness	■ Scheduling a self-care or fun activity each day and sticking to it
	■ Taking a walk or engaging in a hobby during a time typically associated with feelings of sadness
	■ Watching a funny video or musical when feeling down
Frustration/Anger	■ Losing in a game or activity
	■ Having to work at solving a problem or puzzle that is extremely challenging or has no solution
	■ Having to complete a "boring" task
Guilt/Shame	■ Talking to someone else about something that brings up embarrassment or shame
	■ Apologizing to someone (if guilt is justified)

not only anxiety but also sadness, frustration, anger, and even guilt or shame. Your child may struggle with one emotion much more than others, and in that case, most of the items on your child's *Emotional Behavior Form* would likely be situations that elicited that one emotion. However, if your child struggles with experiencing a range of intense emotions, your child's *Emotional Behavior Form* may include situations that bring up several different emotions. Regardless of which strong emotions cause your child the most difficulty, situational emotion exposures can help!

Many parents find it helpful to see examples of some different situational emotional exposures that their child may complete to learn to tolerate and cope with different types of emotions. Table 16.2: *Exposure Examples for Different Problem Areas* lists some examples of potential exposures for addressing various types of emotions and problem areas. As you review the examples in this table, try to think about some possible exposures your child could complete for the different situations on his or her *Emotional Behavior Form*.

Safety Behaviors and What to Do About Them

When approaching a difficult situation, both children and adults rely from time to time on certain objects, people, or behaviors to help themselves feel safer or reduce their distress. For example, maybe you recall that as a child you carried your favorite blanket or stuffed animal to school or stores in order to feel more comfortable. As an adult, maybe you avoid attending work parties unless you know in advance that certain coworkers will be there, or you bury your head in your phone in certain social situations so that you look busy and feel less awkward. All of these are examples of common **safety behaviors** that many people use to feel safe, reduce distress, or tolerate situations more comfortably. Safety behaviors can be objects or people your child relies on in a situation in order to feel safe, or they can be subtle behaviors your child uses to distract from the situation and the strong emotions it elicits. The examples discussed above and others like them are usually unproblematic and typically don't interfere with the day-to-day functioning of most people. However, some children with emotional disorders come to rely upon safety behaviors in order to get through difficult situations, turning the behaviors themselves into a problem.

Why are safety behaviors a problem? One reason is that your child may come to believe that he or she can only approach or tolerate a difficult situation by using a safety behavior, as past experience has taught him or her to associate a particular object or person with safety. For example, imagine that your child gets very nervous about attending her gymnastics class due to fears of other children watching her and fears of getting hurt. As a result, your child asks you to stay near her for the entire class. You agree to stay, and of course your child completes the class without incident. However, your child may have learned that gymnastics class is safe only when mom or dad is there, assuming that nothing bad or upsetting happened just because you attended. In other words, your child learned to attribute the lack of a negative outcome to the presence of the safety behavior (you). What do you think might happen the next time you are unable to stay for class? There is a good chance your child may become very upset because she believes that if you leave, something bad may happen. Giving up the safety behavior has suddenly become very difficult!

Another reason why safety behaviors are a problem is because they prevent your child from fully attending to or experiencing parts of the situation that contradict your child's fears or beliefs about what might happen. For example, if your child avoids making eye contact when meeting someone new, he might fail to notice that the person is smiling and appears friendly. As a result, your child may continue to believe that others dislike him. Or if your child distracts himself or herself during a thunderstorm by hiding under a blanket and listening to music on headphones, he or she is not able to learn that the wind is not actually strong enough to blow the house down or that the thunder, while loud, is not dangerous.

So how should you handle safety behaviors that your child may use during exposure? First, you should be on the lookout for these safety behaviors, including subtle avoidance behaviors like distraction or not attending fully to the exposure. Your child may not be aware that he or she is using a safety behavior and, if you gently point it out during exposure and suggest that your child do something different, your child may readily comply with minimal distress. However, giving up some safety behaviors might cause your child so much distress that he or she would be unable or unwilling to enter the situation at all without them. In such a case, a useful first step may be to try the exposure with the safety behavior, and then, once your child has accomplished that step, gradually work on phasing out the safety behavior in future exposure steps.

Using Your Opposite Parenting Behaviors to Support Exposures

By the end of this session, you and your child should have a very good idea of which exposures your child will begin with and when your child might complete them. But what should *you* do before, during, and after the exposure? Fortunately, you have now learned four different opposite parenting behaviors that can also be used to help support your child's exposures. Take a look at Table 16.3: *How to Use Opposite Parenting Behaviors to Support Exposures* for ideas about how these behaviors might come in handy during your child's exposures.

For your home learning assignment this week, you will complete Worksheet 16.3: *Using Opposite Parenting Behaviors to Support Exposures at Home.* Use this worksheet to indicate the exposure step your child completes over the next week, as well as how you used each of the opposite emotional parenting behaviors to support your child during his or her exposure.

Emotion Ladder for Breaking Down Exposures

As you are beginning to plan exposures with your child and your child's therapist, you may discover that some of the items on the *Emotional Behavior Form—Child Version* you and your child collaborated on may actually need to be broken down into multiple exposure steps. You can use the *Emotion Ladder* (Form 16.3) to break down each situation on the *Emotional Behavior Form—Child Version* into smaller, more approachable steps that progress toward the larger goal of approaching and sticking with each situation without using unhelpful emotional behaviors. You will find space on the *Emotion Ladder* to indicate the reward you and your child have decided that he or she will earn for completing each step. Keep in mind that you do not need to fill out each and every rung of the ladder on the *Emotion Ladder*; rather, use as many steps as necessary in order to help your child approach the larger goal or situation. With the help of the group leaders, you might use this *Emotion Ladder* to begin to break down a situation from the Emotional Behavior Form—Child Version in preparation for next session's exposures, which may take place at a community location. Additionally, when you reconvene with your child at the end of the child portion of this session, you will work together with your child and his or her therapist to come up with ideas for your child's

Table 16.3 How to Use Opposite Parenting Behaviors to Support Exposures

Opposite Parenting Behavior	How to Use It During Exposures
Expressing Empathy	▪ Express empathy (and encouragement) before and during the exposure, especially if your child is struggling to approach or stay in the situation. **Example: "I know how difficult this must be because your fear of dogs is very strong, but you have the Emotion Detective skills now to do it!"**
Consistent Use of Reinforcement and Discipline	▪ When you and your child plan to do an exposure, make sure you follow through with the plan (even if just some small part of the plan!). ▪ Use labeled praise to praise your child after the exposure. Even if your child needs to complete something easier than what was planned, or if your child was unable to complete the exposure at all, find something to praise. **Example: "I was so impressed with how you smiled and said 'hello' to that waitress!"** **Example: "I know your sad feelings made it really difficult to take a walk today like we planned. Thanks for giving it a try—we can try again tomorrow."** ▪ Plan rewards your child can earn for completing exposures, and provide rewards as soon after exposure completion as possible.
Healthy Independence-Granting	▪ Allow your child to participate in choosing which exposure step to complete next and when to do it. ▪ If your child appears to be having difficulty approaching the exposure, express empathy and encouragement and then **wait** to allow your child sufficient opportunity to begin. ▪ Allow your child to complete exposures on his or her own whenever possible, without stepping in to help.
Healthy Emotional Modeling	▪ Communicate with your words, expression, and behaviors that the situation your child is approaching is safe. ▪ It may be helpful to complete the exposure before or with your child to let your child know that the exposure is safe. However, doing this all the time may result in you becoming a safety behavior. ▪ If you believe your own emotions might get in the way of your child's exposures, talk to your child's therapist about how to address this.

Use this form to identify and describe situations that cause your child to feel strong emotions, as well as the emotional behaviors your child uses in these situations. Using the Emotion Thermometer below, rate how much uncomfortable *emotion* your child experiences in each situation. When creating this list, think of unhelpful behaviors like avoidance, escape, or other undesired actions (like aggression) that you hope may change during treatment. You and your child can use the last column (Did you work on it?) to see how much progress your child has made on these behaviors over time.

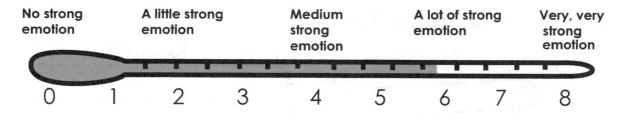

Situation	Emotional Behavior	How strong is the emotion (0-8)?	Did you work on it (Y/N)?
Reading aloud in Spanish class	Avoiding class, reading very quickly	7	
Being alone in crowds of people	Avoiding crowded places	6	
Asking a friend to come over and play	Avoiding talking about it, Ask mom to do it for me	6	
Playing volleyball in gym class	Skip gym, Pretend I'm hurt	5	
Feeling frustrated about math homework	Put it off, Ignore it and don't finish it	4	
Being around dogs	Stay away from places where there are dogs	4	
Things being unfair	Yell, Throw things	3	
Worry about getting lost in a mall or a store	Stay close to mom, Hold mom's hand the whole time, Avoid going to malls	3	
Having to talk to strangers in stores or restaurants	Ask parents to talk for me	3	
Asking my teacher a question about something	Avoid my teacher, Pretend I know how to do the work	2	

Figure 16.6

Sample Emotional Behavior Form

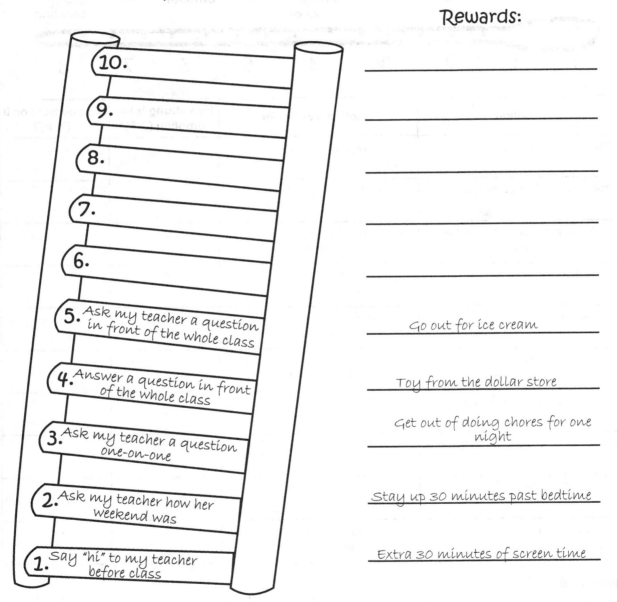

Goal: _Ask my teacher a question in front of the whole class._

One Step at a Time:

Rewards:

10.

9.

8.

7.

6.

5. _Ask my teacher a question in front of the whole class_ — _Go out for ice cream_

4. _Answer a question in front of the whole class_ — _Toy from the dollar store_

3. _Ask my teacher a question one-on-one_ — _Get out of doing chores for one night_

2. _Ask my teacher how her weekend was_ — _Stay up 30 minutes past bedtime_

1. _Say "hi" to my teacher before class_ — _Extra 30 minutes of screen time_

Figure 16.7

Sample Emotion Ladder

version of the Emotion Ladder for this week's home learning assignment (Form 10.1: *My Emotion Ladder for Home Learning* in the child portion of the workbook).

Many parents find it helpful to see both a sample completed *Emotional Behavior Form* and a sample *Emotion Ladder* to understand how these forms can be used together to facilitate exposures. We have included a *Sample Emotional Behavior Form* (Figure 16.6) for you to review, as well as a *Sample Emotion Ladder* (Figure 16.7) that breaks the lowest item on the *Sample Emotional Behavior Form* into smaller, more approachable steps.

Form 16.3: Emotion Ladder

Goal: _____

_____

One Step at a Time:

Rewards:

Worksheet 16.3: Using Opposite Parenting Behaviors to Support Exposures at Home

During this treatment, you have been learning about four different parenting behaviors that research has shown to be less helpful in managing your child's strong emotions and emotional behaviors. We call them **emotional parenting behaviors** because many parents use these behaviors when they themselves are feeling strong emotions. You have also learned about four **opposite parenting behaviors** to use instead that are typically more helpful for managing your child's emotions and behaviors. This week, your job is to use at least one of these opposite parenting behaviors to support your child in completing planned exposure(s) at home. Use the spaces below to indicate the exposure your child completed and how you used one or more of the opposite parenting behaviors to help your child be successful.

The Exposure My Child Completed Was:	
How I expressed empathy:	
How I practiced consistency:	
How I granted my child independence:	
How I modeled healthy emotion expression and effective coping:	

- To learn what to expect as your child begins exposure
- To learn how to manage common challenges that arise during exposure

What to Expect as Your Child Begins Exposure

During these next four sessions, your child will be completing a variety of experiments—which we have been calling situational emotion exposures—to see what happens when he or she approaches and sticks with the situations on the *Emotional Behavior Form—Child Version* without using unhelpful emotional behaviors. We think that you will find these sessions to be some of the most helpful, exciting, and encouraging ones in this entire treatment, both for you and for your child. Your child will be approaching situations he or she hasn't approached in a long time (or maybe even ever!), using Emotion Detective skills to cope with emotions and situations in new ways, and practicing new and more helpful behaviors in difficult situations. Many parents see their child doing things they never thought possible in these sessions, and children begin to feel an incredible sense of accomplishment and self-efficacy as they learn to get through and manage difficult situations and emotions more effectively.

All that being said, it is also very common for some children to experience a brief and temporary increase in distress, anxiety, or frustration as they first begin exposures. This response actually makes a lot of sense! You and your child's therapist are asking your child to approach and sit with uncomfortable emotions he or she has been avoiding for a long time, and to change the way he or she behaves in situations that elicit distress. Although your child may be very motivated to feel less anxious or sad or angry overall, your child may nevertheless have difficulty feeling motivated for some exposures, and when in distress your child may have difficulty remembering why sticking with an exposure is important. You should also keep in mind that exposures are totally new to your child! We are asking your child to do something very scary or difficult with the promise that things will become easier over the longer term, but your child may not have experienced these changes yet. Once your child begins to recognize how exposures are helping reduce feelings of distress over the longer term and increasing his or her ability to cope with difficult situations, his or her willingness and intrinsic motivation to complete exposures will likely improve.

Until that happens, *what can you do to support your child?* Perhaps the most important thing you can do is stick with the exposures planned by you and your child's therapist, even if your child initially seems to experience an increase in distress. Remind yourself that your child is learning new ways to approach and behave in emotional situations, and your child may seem a bit more uncomfortable for a couple weeks until these behaviors become more routine. You should also continue to practice using your opposite parenting behaviors to support your child's exposures:

- When you feel frustrated or critical of your child, use the opposite parenting behavior of **expressing empathy** to communicate that you understand your child's strong emotions and desire to avoid an exposure.

- When you feel like backing out of an exposure because you are tired or your child appears overwhelmed, consider how you can continue to be **consistent** with your child at home while still empathizing with his or her emotions.

- When your child is struggling with an exposure and you are struggling with watching your child in distress, consider how you can help him or her to approach or complete the exposure **independently**. In other words, you may need to remind yourself during more difficult exposures that your child is safe and that any distress he or she displays does not necessarily mean he or she is in danger or needs you to intervene.

- When you yourself have the impulse to avoid or ignore situations that bring up strong emotions for you, notice this impulse and consider how you might practice **healthy emotional modeling** in front of your child instead.

And finally, be sure to consistently reward your child for completing exposures, using the rewards on the *My Emotion Ladder*. Remember— your child may lack the motivation inside himself or herself to approach and complete exposures, and consistent rewards are especially important at this stage!

For your home learning assignments during these sessions, you should use Form 16.4: *Situational Emotion Exposure Tracking Form* to record details about each exposure your child completes at home, your child's response to the exposure, and your parenting behaviors during the exposure. Bring this form to each session so that you can review it with your child's therapist. This form is particularly important to complete if you run into any challenges during these home-based exposures.

Managing Common Exposure Challenges

By now, both you and your child have done quite a bit of careful planning for exposures. You have now thought a lot about the types of situations that are challenging for your child, the emotional behaviors he or she uses in those situations, and how to craft exposures that involve practicing different behaviors in these situations. You and your child have also considered the relative difficulty of these different exposures and how to break them down into smaller, achievable, concrete steps using the *Emotion Ladders* for situational emotion exposure practice found within the child section of this workbook (Forms 11.1–11.4). All of this preparation should set you and your child up for a successful experience with exposures. However, challenges may still arise with exposures, and it is important to anticipate and prepare for them so that you are not caught by surprise if they do happen. Here are some common challenges that may come up during exposures, as well as some suggestions for effective strategies to manage them:

- **What if an exposure turns out to be too easy for my child?**
  This is often a good problem to encounter! It may occur because children sometimes have difficulty predicting how much emotion they will feel in a given situation, or because the lessons your child has learned during earlier exposures have carried over into other types of situations (something called **generalization**). You can handle this situation by either doing something to make the current exposure more difficult (e.g., if the task is to say "hello" to a stranger, encourage your child to follow up the greeting with a question) or by moving through the next several steps on the ladder more quickly. An exposure turning out to be easier than anticipated may also be a sign that it's time to re-rate, or even eliminate, some of the items on your child's *Emotional Behavior Form*. There is another copy of the form at the end of this chapter in case you need to work with your child and your therapist to

create a revised *Emotional Behavior Form* (Form 16.5). One final possibility is that your child may be using safety behaviors during the exposure in order to avoid or distract from the emotions he or she is experiencing in the situation. Consider whether your child might be relying on things, people, distractions, or other subtle avoidance behaviors to get through the situation, and make a plan to gradually reduce or eliminate your child's use of these safety behaviors.

■ **What if an exposure turns out to be too difficult for my child?** Most parents will run into this issue at some point, and it can result in significant anxiety and feelings of helplessness for the parent. One of the most important things to remember about exposures is that, whenever possible, you should not allow your child to escape or avoid an exposure entirely, as this can actually increase distress and the likelihood of engaging in emotional behaviors the next time your child attempts the exposure. Your first line of attack is always to try using all of your opposite parenting behaviors to encourage your child to complete the exposure. In other words, express empathy, remind your child of the promised reward, and remain consistent in your expectations. Sometimes if you use these parenting behaviors and wait long enough, your child will actually complete the exposure. However, if your child is still in extreme distress or you become concerned that you may run out of time waiting for your child to approach the situation, it may be time to consider modifying the planned exposure to improve your child's chance of success. For example, if the planned exposure is for your child to say "hello" to a stranger, you can consider asking your child to smile at or make eye contact with a stranger instead. If the planned exposure is to take a walk around the neighborhood with you and your child is refusing to get out of bed, you can consider encouraging your child to get out of bed and sit with you in the backyard instead. Remember that the goal is for your child to complete some aspect of the exposure, even if your child is unable to complete exactly what was planned.

■ **What if my child does not report a decrease in anxiety, sadness, or frustration during the exposure?** Although your child's level of strong emotion will often decrease over the course of an exposure, this does not always happen. When it doesn't happen, parents and children may feel discouraged or may wonder if exposure is working. However, it's important to remember that a decrease in emotion during a single exposure is only **one** of several ways exposures are thought to work. Remind your child that he or she was able to get through the situation or experience the strong emotion without using emotional behaviors, even if it was very difficult! Remind your child that the bad thing he or she expected to happen did not actually occur, or that it wasn't as bad as your child thought. You may also want to consider repeating the same exposure several times on different occasions, taking opportunities to point out if your child's level of emotion decreases with repeated practice.

- **What if something goes wrong during the exposure or something bad happens?** Exposures do not always go exactly as planned. Unexpected things may happen, or one of your child's feared outcomes may actually turn out to be true. This is especially true when your child is completing exposures that involve other people, but it is also true with exposures involving weather, animals, or other unpredictable events or situations. The world can be an unpredictable place and we cannot always protect children in exposures or outside of them from, for example, a dog licking them or a waiter making a strange face at a whispered request. However, by changing the way you think about unexpected events like these that may occur during exposure, you can turn them into opportunities. In the end, exposures can actually help your child learn to tolerate the uncertainty inherent in the world. Obviously, you do not want to intentionally ask your child to approach situations you believe will not turn out well, but it is perfectly okay and even sometimes desirable to not be certain about the outcome of an exposure. And if one of your child's feared outcomes does occur, this is a great opportunity to help your child use Emotion Detective skills to see that the outcome was probably not as bad as he or she thought it would be, and your child was able to cope with it!

Although we have tried to address some of the common challenges parents face during exposure, there are likely others we did not address. Be sure to discuss unexpected challenges that come up with your child's therapist during the remainder of the E section of treatment.

Form 16.4: Situational Emotion Exposure Tracking Form

Use this form over the next four sessions (and even beyond!) to record the exposures your child completes. This form is particularly helpful for tracking information about your child's progress and about your own behaviors and responses during exposures.

Exposure	Child's Highest Level of Emotion	Safety Behaviors or Other Emotional Behaviors Your Child Used	Emotional Parenting Behaviors You Used	Opposite Parenting Behaviors You Used

(continued)

Form 16.4: Continued

Exposure	Child's Highest Level of Emotion	Safety Behaviors or Other Emotional Behaviors Your Child Used	Emotional Parenting Behaviors You Used	Opposite Parenting Behaviors You Used

Form 16.5: Emotional Behavior Form

As your child completes more and more situational emotion exposures, you may discover that your original form seems out of date. Maybe situations that originally seemed difficult to your child now feel easy, or maybe your child has already successfully approached all of the situations on his or her first form. Or maybe what you and your child want to work on has changed! Use this form to identify and describe the situations that **now** cause your child to feel strong emotions, as well as the emotional behaviors your child uses in these situations. Using the Emotion Thermometer below, rate how much uncomfortable *emotion* your child experiences in each situation.

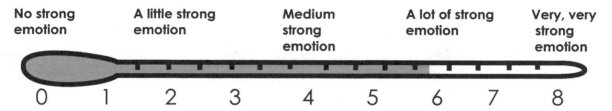

| No strong emotion | A little strong emotion | Medium strong emotion | A lot of strong emotion | Very, very strong emotion |

0   1   2   3   4   5   6   7   8

Situation	Emotional Behavior	How strong is the emotion (0–8)?	Did you work on it (Y/N)?

CHAPTER 17

Stay Healthy and Happy
for Parents

(Session 15 for Parents)

SESSION 15 GOALS

- To review Emotion Detective skills and opposite parenting behaviors
- To create a plan for sustaining and continuing progress after treatment
- To learn how to identify and address the warning signs of relapse

Review of Emotion Detective Skills

Congratulations on reaching the end of treatment—this is no small feat! For the past weeks, your child has been working hard to learn new Emotion Detective skills for noticing, understanding, and changing his or her emotional responses to difficult situations. As your child's parent, you have also been working hard to observe and understand your child's emotions and your own reactions to them, as well as to adjust the parenting strategies that you use when your child experiences strong emotions. We hope that these skills are beginning to feel natural for both you and your child. Table 17.1: *Emotion Detective Skills (CLUES)* reviews the major skills that your child and you learned in each section of this treatment.

Although your child is likely using many of these skills quite successfully and independently by now, it is not uncommon for children to use certain skills more than others or to require more help practicing certain skills. For example, your child may be very good at recognizing when he is falling into a thinking trap but may still have difficulty independently using the steps of Detective Thinking to get himself out of it. Alternatively, your child may be

Table 17.1 Emotion Detective Skills (CLUES)

	Skills My Child Learned	Skills I Learned
C Skill **Consider How I Feel**	■ Three parts of an emotion ■ Acting opposite experiments ■ Body scanning ■ Sensational exposures	■ Emotional and opposite parenting behaviors ■ Using positive reinforcement ■ Expressing empathy
L Skill **Look at My Thoughts**	■ Identifying thinking traps	■ Different types of reinforcement and punishment ■ Using consistent discipline and praise
U Skill **Use Detective Thinking and Problem Solving**	■ Detective Thinking ■ Problem Solving	■ Healthy independence-granting ■ Shaping Detective Thinking and Problem Solving
E Skill **Experience My Emotions**	■ Present-moment awareness ■ Nonjudgmental awareness ■ Situational emotion exposures	■ Healthy emotional modeling ■ Using opposite parenting behaviors to support exposure

very good at using body scanning to identify body clues but may struggle to identify thoughts that are contributing to her feelings of anxiety or sadness. Children are different from one another, and they learn and master skills at very different paces. Aside from these differences *between* children, individual children may use skills inconsistently or may successfully use them in one type of emotional situation but struggle to use them in others. For example, your child may be successfully using present-moment awareness skills to just notice and experience feelings of anxiety without acting on them, but he or she may have great difficulty doing the same for feelings of anger.

Therefore, it is important to remember that ALL children can and should continue to improve in their mastery of the Emotion Detective skills after treatment. You can help your child continue to build mastery with these skills by first considering which ones he or she is already using quite well, and which ones your child needs your help to practice more consistently and understand more thoroughly. Use Worksheet 17.1: *Reviewing Your Child's Emotion Detective Skills* to note situations in which your child is currently using each of the skills, as well as to rate your child's effectiveness in using each skill. Use this worksheet in the future to help your child develop the lower-rated skills more fully.

Just as your child likely has strengths and weaknesses in his or her ability to use the different types of Emotion Detective skills, you probably have strengths and weaknesses in your ability to consistently apply the different opposite parenting behaviors reviewed across sessions. Expressing empathy might come quite naturally to you, for example, but being consistent with discipline and reinforcement might require much more concerted effort! Use Worksheet 17.2: *Reviewing Your Opposite Parenting Behaviors* to identify situations in which you are practicing each of the four opposite parenting behaviors, as well as situations in which you believe you could attempt to use these opposite parenting behaviors in helpful ways.

Creating a Progress Plan

Just as many children have skills that require continued practice after treatment, most children still struggle with strong emotions from time to time or still use some unhelpful emotional behaviors. We hope that you have noticed some significant and encouraging changes in your child's awareness of his or her emotions, reactions to his or her emotions, and willingness to approach and sit with emotional situations. Despite these changes, there is likely still more work to be done. Fortunately, both you and your child now have the skills you need to work as a detective team on these remaining situations or areas where strong emotions and behaviors still get in the way! In order to do this, you and your child must first identify these problem situations or areas.

Work with your group leaders to identify three remaining problem areas and to create three goals around each problem area, using Worksheet 17.3: *Supporting Your Emotion Detective After Treatment*. For example, perhaps your child is now successful at using present-moment awareness skills to notice (but not act) on anger when participating in sports with peers at school, but has difficulty doing this consistently with siblings. The goal for your child might be to practice just noticing his anger without acting on it when he is playing with siblings. You may wish to consult your Top Problems ratings on the *Weekly Top Problem Progress Form* that your group leaders will review with you in this session and/or the most recent version of your *Emotional Behavior Form*, or other workbook tools to identify these goals.

Next, choose **one** of these goals to work on first after treatment ends. Use the bottom portion of Worksheet 17.3 to plan out five steps your child can take, to work on this one goal, skills your child can use at each step, and opposite parenting behaviors you can use to support your child in achieving each step.

Lapse Versus Relapse: Identifying Warning Signs of Relapse

After treatment ends, you will likely feel a deep sense of relief and accomplishment. After watching your child struggle with strong emotions for so long, and after struggling alongside your child as his or her parent, it can be encouraging to see your child be able to attend school, participate in activities, and socialize without experiencing such intense feelings of anger, anxiety, or sadness. Mixed with these feelings of relief and accomplishment, you may also experience fears or doubts about your child's ability to handle difficult situations independently. It can be very difficult to transition from the feeling of reassurance of knowing that a professional is monitoring and working closely with your child each week to managing your child's symptoms on your own. You may be asking yourself things like: "Is my child really ready to end treatment?"; "What do I do if my child seems to be getting worse?"; "How do I know when it's time to return to treatment?"

You may find that you remain on high alert after treatment ends, carefully monitoring your child's emotional experiences for any signs of difficulty or trouble. This is natural and not necessarily a bad thing! Your child may not notice if his or her emotions are becoming more intense or if he or she is more consistently avoiding certain situations or emotions. Therefore, you *should* be watchful for any significant changes in your child's emotions, behaviors, or functioning. That being said, it is also important that you not jump to conclusions about the meaning of any of these changes. Temporary setbacks are normal and quite common after treatment and typically do not mean that your child must return to therapy.

So how do you know if your child is only experiencing a short-term, temporary setback or more significant difficulties that necessitate a return to treatment? To answer this question, it is helpful to distinguish between a **lapse** and a **relapse**. A lapse is a temporary and short-term return of symptoms that does not typically require further treatment. Rather, a lapse is an indication that your child should review his or her UP-C workbook, return to practicing his or her Emotion Detective skills, and work with you or another adult to make a plan for facing and sticking with the situations that are causing trouble. A relapse, on the other hand, is a longer-term, more significant return of symptoms that typically causes noticeable difficulties for your child. A relapse is a sign that you should contact your child's therapist and discuss whether a return to treatment is necessary.

If you have questions about whether your child is experiencing a lapse or a relapse, Table 17.2 might provide some clarity. For each category in the table, consider whether your child's symptoms fall into the "lapse" or the "relapse" category. The more symptoms that fall into the "relapse" category, the more strongly you should consider contacting your child's therapist to discuss a return to treatment.

Table 17.2 Lapse Versus Relapse

	Lapse	Relapse
Length of Symptoms	Brief (e.g., several days to a week) period of increased symptoms	Prolonged (e.g., several weeks or more) period of increased symptoms
Frequency of Symptoms	Occasionally experiences strong emotions or uses emotional behaviors (e.g., once or twice per week)	Frequently experiences strong emotions or uses emotional behaviors (e.g., every day or almost every day)
Intensity of Emotions	Emotions are mostly of mild to moderate intensity, with occasional strong emotions	Emotions are mostly of moderate to strong intensity
Frequency of Avoidance or Other Emotional Behaviors	Uses avoidance or other very problematic emotional behaviors infrequently (e.g., once per week or less)	Uses avoidance or other very problematic emotional behaviors more than once per week
Types of Emotional Behaviors Used	When using emotional behaviors, typically uses distraction or more subtle forms of avoidance	When using emotional behaviors, typically tries to escape or withdraw, or uses verbal/physical aggression
Ability to Recover from Minor Setbacks	Has minor setbacks but is able to use Emotion Detective skills to approach and stick with difficult situations the next time around	Has setbacks that result in difficulty approaching and sticking with similar situations the next time around
Interference and Distress Caused by Symptoms	Symptoms cause minimal to moderate levels of distress and do not impact daily functioning in any significant way	Symptoms are very distressing and/or create impairments in daily functioning
Recall and Use of Skills	Recalls skills from treatment and is able to use them effectively when difficult situations arise, with minimal prompting from parents	Has difficulty recalling treatment skills, has difficulty applying them in different situations, and/or requires parents to heavily coach the skill each time

Over the past 15 sessions, you and your child have worked hard to learn the skills needed to form a powerful and capable detective team at home. We hope that you and your child have not only learned a lot about the benefits of approaching and sticking with emotions, but have had fun doing so! You and your child may still have some difficult work ahead of you, but it is important to celebrate all the difficult work you have already done and the amazing things your child has accomplished. Thank you for participating in this treatment, and welcome to the Emotion Detective family!

Worksheet 17.1: Reviewing Your Child's Emotion Detective Skills

Emotion Detective Skill	Situations Where My Child Uses this Skill	How Effective is My Child in Using this Skill?
Identifying the three parts of an emotion		Rating (0-8): _____
Acting opposite to difficult emotions		Rating (0-8): _____
Body scanning		Rating (0-8): _____
Detective thinking		Rating (0-8): _____
Problem solving		Rating (0-8): _____
Present-moment and nonjudgmental awareness		Rating (0-8): _____

0   1   2   3   4   5   6   7   8

Not Effective   Very Effective

Worksheet 17.2: Reviewing Your Opposite Parenting Behaviors

Emotional Parenting Behavior	Opposite Parenting Behavior	Situation Where I Am Using this Opposite Parenting Behavior	Situations Where I Could Work on Using this Opposite Parenting Behavior
Overcontrol/ Overprotection	Healthy Independence-Granting		
Criticism	Expressing Empathy & Positive Reinforcement		
Inconsistent Reinforcement & Discipline	Consistent Reinforcement & Discipline		
Excessive Emotional Modeling	Healthy Emotional Modeling		

Worksheet 17.3: Supporting Your Emotion Detective after Treatment

We hope that your Emotion Detective is less bothered by strong emotions now and is engaging in fewer emotional behaviors. Even though your child has undoubtedly made a lot of progress, more often than not children still have things to work on after treatment ends. This worksheet will help you identify what those things are and how to work on them. Identify **the three most important goals** for your child to work toward after treatment ends, and write these goals in the spaces below. Then use the bottom of the page to identify steps your child can take toward one of these goals, skills your child can use to complete each step, and the opposite parenting behaviors you can use to support your child.

Goal #1	
Goal #2	
Goal #3	

Steps My Child Can Take Toward One of These Goals	Skills My Child Can Use to Complete Each Step	Opposite Parenting Behaviors I Can Use and Other Ways I Can Support My Child with Each Step
1)		
2)		
3)		
4)		
5)		

Jill Ehrenreich-May, PhD, is the Director of the Child and Adolescent Mood and Anxiety Treatment (CAMAT) program and Associate Professor in the Child Division of the Department of Psychology at the University of Miami. In addition to the development and evaluation of evidence-based treatment approaches for anxiety and depressive disorders in youth, she is particularly interested in clinician training and the dissemination and implementation of effective treatments in environments that maximize their impact and benefit for children. Her current research has been supported by grants from the National Institute of Mental Health and the Children's Trust.

Sarah M. Kennedy, PhD, is a postdoctoral fellow at Children's Hospital Colorado, where she provides clinical services and conducts research on transdiagnostic approaches to assessment and treatment of emotional disorders in youth. She has published numerous book chapters and articles on the etiology and treatment of emotional disorders in children and adolescents.

Jamie A. Sherman, MS, is a doctoral candidate in the child clinical psychology program at the University of Miami. Clinically, she is interested in providing effective treatment for youth with a variety of anxiety and mood concerns. Her research focuses on the development and evaluation of evidence-supported treatments for pediatric mood and anxiety disorders.

Emily L. Bilek, PhD, is a Clinical Assistant Professor at the University of Michigan in the Department of Psychiatry. Her research interests include the investigation of treatment mechanisms and treatment enhancement for cognitive behavioral therapies, and treatment deployment and dissemination.

David H. Barlow, PhD, ABPP, is Professor of Psychiatry and Psychology Emeritus at Boston University and the Founder and Director of the Center for Anxiety and Related Disorders, Emeritus. He has received numerous awards and has published over 600 articles and chapters and over 80 books, and his research has been continuously funded by the National Institutes of Health for over 45 years. He is editor- in- chief for the Treatments *That Work* series of therapist manuals and patient workbooks for Oxford University Press.

Printed in the USA/Agawam, MA
July 26, 2022

796200.060